Table of Contents

D0470672

Introduction

The Stories

Types of stories:
- Folk and Fairy Tales
- Myths and Legends
- Realistic Fiction
- Nonfiction
- Poetry

Stories span from mid-second to beginning fourth grade reading levels and can be used in several ways:

1. As directed lessons
   - with small groups of students reading at the same level
   - with an individual student
2. For partner reading
3. For independent practice
   - at school
   - at home

Determine your purpose for selecting a story — instructional device, partner reading, or independent reading. Each purpose calls for a different degree of story difficulty.

A single story can be used for more than one purpose. You might first use the story as an instructional tool, have partners read the story a second time for greater fluency, and then use it at a later time for independent reading.

When presenting a story to a group or individual student, discuss any vocabulary that might be difficult to decode or understand.

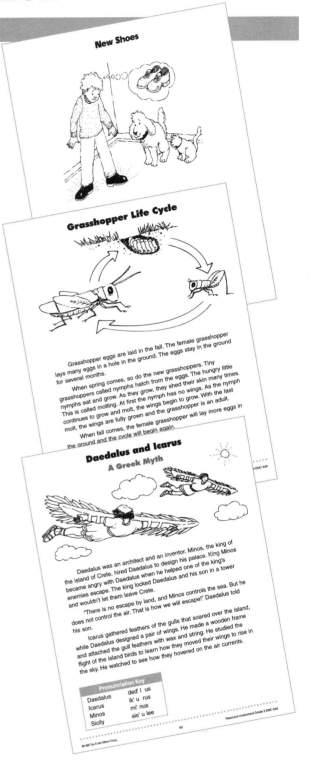

Each story is followed by five pages of activities covering a variety of reading skills:

- **Comprehension** - recall story details, draw conclusions, make inferences & predictions, sequence events, generalize, compare & contrast
- **Vocabulary** - word definitions, multiple-meaning words, figurative language, antonyms, synonyms, homophones
- **Phonetic elements**
- **Word attack** - base words, suffixes, prefixes, compound words, contractions, syllables, possessive forms
- **Parts of speech** - nouns, verbs, adjectives, pronouns, adverbs
- **Record information** - list, categorize, personal narrative

Several students may read the same story but need to practice different skills. Provide each reader with the task that is appropriate for his/her needs.

Skills pages can be used more than one time.

1. As directed mini-lessons with a small group or with an individual student:
   - Make a transparency for students to follow as you work through the lesson, or
   - Write the activity on the chalkboard and call on students to fill in the answers as a group, or
   - Reproduce the page for everyone to use as you go through the lesson.

2. As independent practice:
   Independent practice should be on skills already introduced to the reader. Review directions and be sure the student understands what is to be done. Go over the completed assignment with the student to determine if further practice is needed.

New Shoes

My shoes are new and squeaky shoes,

They're very shiny, creaky shoes.

I wish I had my leaky shoes

That mother threw away.

I liked my old brown leaky shoes

Much better than these creaky shoes,

These shiny, creaky, squeaky shoes

I've got to wear today.

Anonymous

. . . . New Shoes . . . .

Name _____

Questions About *New Shoes*

1. What words were used to describe the new shoes?

   _____

2. What words were used to describe the old shoes?

   _____

3. Why do you think Mother threw away the old shoes?

   _____

4. Why do you think the child wanted the old shoes back?

   _____

5. Which words in this poem rhyme with...?

   squeaky _____

   away _____

Think About It

Design a machine to remove the "squeak" from new shoes.
Draw a picture of your machine.

Explain how it works.

   _____

   _____

Name _____

What Does It Mean?

Write the word or words from the story that mean:

1. letting water in   _____

2. bright and sparkling   _____

3. making a noise   _____

                                         _____

4. contraction for they are _____

5. contraction for I have   _____

6. opposite of new   _____

7. to have on   _____

8. get rid of   _____

9. want   _____

Word Box				
shiny	they're	old	I've	throw away
wear	leaky	wish	creaky	squeaky

On My Feet

List types of shoes and other things you can wear on your feet.

1. _____   7. _____

2. _____   8. _____

3. _____   9. _____

4. _____   10. _____

5. _____   11. _____

6. _____   12. _____

Name _____

Words Beginning with *thr*

Fill in the letters **thr**. Then use the words to complete the sentences.

_____ew   _____ee   _____ush

_____oat   _____ead   _____eat

_____ough   _____ill   _____ob

1. Kim has a sore _____.

2. Sid _____ the ball to Marcus.

3. Mom used a needle and _____ to mend the rip.

4. The bus went _____ a long tunnel.

5. My cat Whiskers will be _____ on Sunday.

6. A _____ was chirping in the apple tree.

eak Word Family

A word family is made of words that are the same except for the beginning sounds. The words **squeaky**, **creaky**, and **leaky** are in the same word family.

Use the following clues to help you find more members of the **eak** word family.

1. mountain top   *p*_____eak   5. noise a mouse makes   _____eak

2. creep up   _____eak   6. let water in   _____eak

3. bird's bill   _____eak   7. talk   _____eak

4. not strong   _____eak   8. noise an old door makes   _____eak

Name _____

Homophones

Homophones are words that sound the same.
They are not spelled the same.
They have different meanings.

Write the homophone on the line.

byte	dough	rain
bear	flee	scent
bury	maize	through

1. bare ___*bear*___   4. threw _____   7. bite _____

2. sent _____   5. berry _____   8. doe _____

3. flea _____   8. rein _____   9. maze _____

Using Homophones

Circle the correct word.

1. The _____ fell all day.
   (rain)   rein

2. The _____ was eating a black _____.
   bare   bear   bury   berry

3. I was surprised he _____ the answer to the question.
   new   knew

4. The farmer must _____ the seeds before the rain falls.
   sow   sew

5. Soo and Kim helped Grandma make cookie _____.
   dough   doe

6. Mark nailed a _____ on the fence to fix it.
   bored   board

7. She hurt her _____ when she stepped on a nail.
   he'll   heel

8. Angela _____ a letter to her friend.
   sent   scent

Name _____

My Favorite Shoes

Draw your favorite pair of shoes here.

1. Write six words that describe them.

2. Why they are your favorite pair?

Bonus - Write a two-line poem about the shoes.

The Wise Old Woman

A wise old woman lived at the edge of the woods. Her son lived down the path and across the woods. One day she filled a basket with cookies for her son. She started down the path into the woods.

On the way she met a bushy-tailed gray wolf. "I am hungry. I'm going to eat you old woman," barked the wolf.

"Don't eat me now," said the old woman. "I am just skin and bones. When I come back from my son's house, I'll be fatter."

"O.K. I will wait for you," barked the wolf.

The old woman went on down the path. She saw a long, green snake hanging from a tree. "I am hungry. I'm going to eat you, old woman," hissed the snake.

"Don't eat me now," said the old woman. "I am just skin and bones. When I come back from my son's house, I'll be fatter."

"O.K. I will wait for you," hissed the snake.

The old woman went on down the path. She saw a big, black bear on the path. "I am hungry. I'm going to eat you, old woman," growled the bear.

"Don't eat me now," said the old woman. "I am just skin and bones. When I come back from my son's house I will be fatter."

The wise, old woman got to her son's house at lunch time. They ate and ate. Then the old woman took a nap. After her nap she said to her son, "Let's eat the cookies in the basket. Then I must go home."

After the snack the old woman asked, "Son, may I have that giant pumpkin in your garden?" She cut open the giant pumpkin and took out all the seeds. Then she got into the pumpkin and rolled into the woods.

The bear saw the pumpkin rolling in the woods. But he was waiting for the old woman. The snake saw the pumpkin, but he was waiting for the old woman, too. As the pumpkin went past the wolf, it rolled into a big tree. It broke open with a loud "Crack!" The snake, the bear, and the wolf ran over to see what was going on.

"It's the old woman," barked the wolf. "I am going to eat you now."

"No!" hissed the snake. "I am going to eat the old woman."

"No, no!" growled the bear. "She is going to be my dinner."

The wise, old woman looked at them. She said, "The strongest of you can eat me." As the animals began to fight, she ran away home.

Name _____

Questions About *The Wise Old Woman*

1. Where did the old woman live?

_____

2. How did she get to her son's house?

_____

3. Who did she meet on the way? What did they want to do to her?

_____ _____ _____

_____

4. What did she do at her son's house?

_____

5. Why did she want the giant pumpkin?

_____

6. List two wise things the old woman did.

_____

Think About It

How can you tell this story is make-believe?

_____

_____

_____

_____

Name _____

What Does It Mean?

Match the word to its meaning in this story.

old	knows things
wise	place to walk
giant	lived a long time
path	very big
skin and bones	not fat
began	big bunch of trees
broke	along the outside
edge	need food
woods	started
hungry	fell apart

Who Am I?

Who or what do the words tell about?
You may use a word more than one time.

big	gray	long	skin and bones
black	green	old	
bushy-tailed	hungry	wise	

woman	wolf
_____	_____
_____	_____
_____	_____

snake	bear
_____	_____
_____	_____
_____	_____

Name _____

Sounds of g

Write the sound the letter **g** makes in these words.
Write **g** or **j** on the line.

1. got _____g_____

2. giant _____

3. gum _____

4. garden _____

5. edge _____

6. goat _____

7. gem _____

8. girl _____

_____um

_____am _____ar

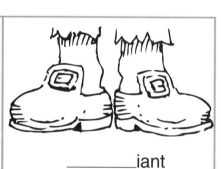

_____iant

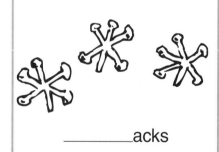

_____acks

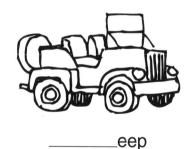

_____eep

_____orilla

Who Owns It?

Put **'s** to show who owns it.

1. the son_'s____ pumpkin

2. old woman_____ basket

3. a wolf_____ bushy-tail

4. pumpkin_____ seeds

5. tree_____ branch

6. black bear_____ paw

Name _____

What Happened Next?

Read, cut, and paste in order.

1.

2.

3.

4.

5.

6.

7.

- -

The old woman got into the giant pumpkin. She rolled into the woods.

The old woman filled a basket with cookies.
She went down the path into the woods.

The pumpkin rolled past the bear, the snake, and the wolf.

The pumpkin rolled into a big tree.
It broke open and the old woman fell out.

She met a wolf, a snake, and a bear.
"Wait until I come back. I'll be fatter," she said.

The old woman ate and took a nap at her son's house.

As the animals began to fight, the old woman ran home.

Name _____

What Did the Old Woman Do?

Circle how the wise old woman solved the problem.

1. The big bear wanted to eat her.
   a. She ran away.
   b. She asked the bear to wait.
   c. She called for help.

2. The old woman had to go through the woods to get home.
   a. She went around the woods.
   b. She had her son go with her.
   c. She got into a pumpkin and rolled into the woods.

3. The pumpkin broke. The wolf, snake, and bear wanted to eat her.
   a. She got them to fight.
   b. She hit them with a big stick.
   c. She paid them to go away.

Draw the animals from the story.

bushy-tailed gray wolf	
big, black bear	long, green snake hanging from a tree

The Messiest Room in Town

Everyone said Herbert's bedroom was the messiest room in town. Everything was covered with toys and clothes (clean and dirty). Pet hair, rotten apple cores, and moldy pizza scraps were on the floor and under the bed. What a mess! Herbert didn't care. He liked his room just the way it was.

Herbert's mother said, "How can you find anything? I'll bet you even have dust bunnies under your bed."

His sister said, "Not dust bunnies, dust monsters. And how do you stand the smell?"

Herbert just grinned and closed the door. "Why do they care about my room?" he thought. "If I put things away, I won't be able to find anything. Besides, it doesn't smell that bad in here."

One night as Herbert was reading in bed, he heard a rumble. Then his bed began to move. He looked up and saw something coming out from under his bed.

Out popped two big brown eyes. Then out came a big brown nose with a clothespin stuck on the end. A dirty brown head poked out and frowned at Herbert. "Herbert," the dust monster said, "this has got to stop. This room has passed messy. It has become a disaster area."

Herbert's only question was, "Why do you have a clothespin on your nose?"

Dust Monster answered, "Because I can't stand the smell of dirty socks and rotten food. It's time to clean up this mess." The monster lurched over to a window and threw it open. "Fresh air at last," sighed Dust Monster.

"Herbert, clean this room up right now. If you don't, I'm going to do something really terrible," shouted the monster. It began to grow bigger and bigger.

Herbert jumped out of bed and began to hang clothes in his closet. He shoved his dirty clothes in a box by the door. He put his toys and books on shelves. As Herbert was working, Dust Monster got smaller and smaller. By the time Herbert was done, the monster was gone. "Wow, I'll never let things get that messy again," said Herbert, and he went to bed.

The next morning everyone was shocked to see how neat and clean his room was. They wanted to know what had happened. Herbert just grinned as he put a "Keep Out" sign on his door.

Name _____

Questions About *The Messiest Room in Town*

1. What made people think Herbert had the messiest room in town?

   _____

2. Why did Herbert's room smell bad?

   _____

3. Why did the dust monster come out from under Herbert's bed?

   _____

4. Why did the dust monster have a clothespin on its nose?

   _____

5. What do you think the dust monster would have done if Herbert didn't clean his room?

   _____

6. How did the bedroom get so messy?

   _____

Think About It

Circle the word that tells about your bedroom.

     messiest room in town   a little messy   neat and clean

How do you clean your room?

_____

_____

Name _____

What Does It Mean?

1. covered with a fuzzy growth
2. small bits of dirt
3. the biggest mess
4. a pin for clothes
5. a noise
6. spoiled
7. very surprised
8. a bad happening
9. moved in a jerky way
10. part of an apple

Word Box

clothespin
core
disaster
dust
lurched
messiest
moldy
rotten
rumble
shocked

n

Read the words in the dark boxes to complete this sentence.

_____ is hiding under the bed.

©1997 by Evan-Moor Corp.

Read and Understand Grade 3 EMC 640

Name _____

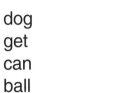

Sounds of Short Vowels

Write each word under the box with its short vowel sound.

dog	that	still	hush	in
get	rock	pup	sing	rest
can	bed	glass	tug	bottle
ball	ring	tell	rattle	of

| a | e | i | o | u |

_____ _____ _____ _____ _____

_____ _____ _____ _____ _____

_____ _____ _____ _____ _____

_____ _____ _____ _____ _____

Add Endings

Add **er** and **est** to each word.
If it ends in **y** - change the **y** to **i** and add the ending.

happy   happiest   happier

        er   **est**

1. small _____smaller_____   _____

2. messy _____   _____

3. funny _____   _____

4. silly _____   _____

5. fast _____   _____

6. tiny _____   _____

Name _____

The Messy Bedroom

1. Circle the pillow on the floor.
   Put an **X** on the pillow on the bed.
2. Color all the footwear brown.
3. Draw an apple core and a half-eaten pizza on the floor.
4. Color clothes red.
5. How many toys do you see? _____
6. List four things that might be under the bed.

_____

Name _____

Read and Draw

Dust Monster crawled out
from under the bed.

Dust Monster threw
open the window.

Herbert was in bed
reading a book.

Herbert put a "Keep Out"
sign on the bedroom door.

Grasshopper Life Cycle

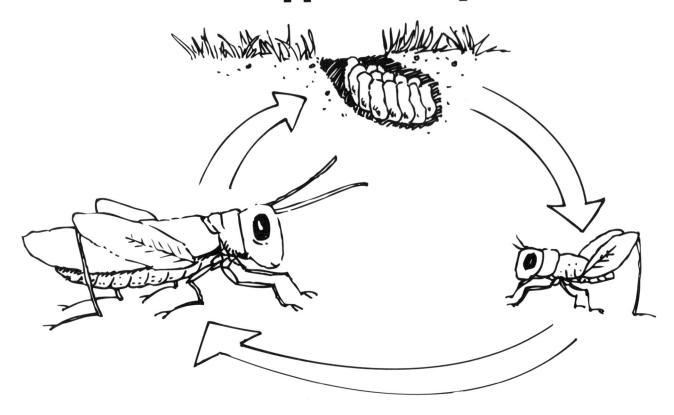

Grasshopper eggs are laid in the fall. The female grasshopper lays many eggs in a hole in the ground. The eggs stay in the ground for several months.

When spring comes, so do the new grasshoppers. Tiny grasshoppers called nymphs hatch from the eggs. The hungry little nymphs eat and grow. As they grow, they shed their skin many times. This is called molting. At first the nymph has no wings. As the nymph continues to grow and molt, the wings begin to grow. With the last molt, the wings are fully grown and the grasshopper is an adult.

When fall comes, the female grasshopper will lay more eggs in the ground and the cycle will begin again.

Name _____

Questions About *Grasshopper Life Cycle*

1. What are the grasshoppers called when they hatch?

   _____

2. Where and when are grasshopper eggs laid?

   _____

3. Who lays the eggs?

   _____

4. Why does a grasshopper shed its skin? What is it called when this happens?

   _____

5. Name the following stages in a grasshopper's life cycle.

_____	_____	_____

6. Why do you think this is called a life **cycle**?

   _____

   _____

Think About It

This story was about the life cycle of a grasshopper. We have a life cycle too. Think about what the stages of a human life cycle might be. Write the stages here.

_____

_____

_____

Name _____

What Happened Next?

Number the pictures in order.
Write a sentence about what happens at each stage.

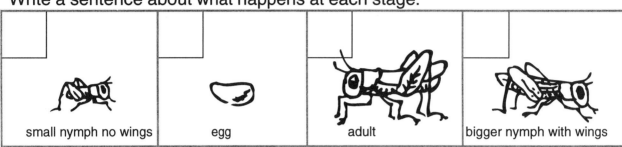

| small nymph no wings | egg | adult | bigger nymph with wings |

1. _____

2. _____

3. _____

4. _____

Parts of a Grasshopper

Here are the parts of a moth.

A grasshopper has the same parts as a moth.
Label the parts of the grasshopper below.

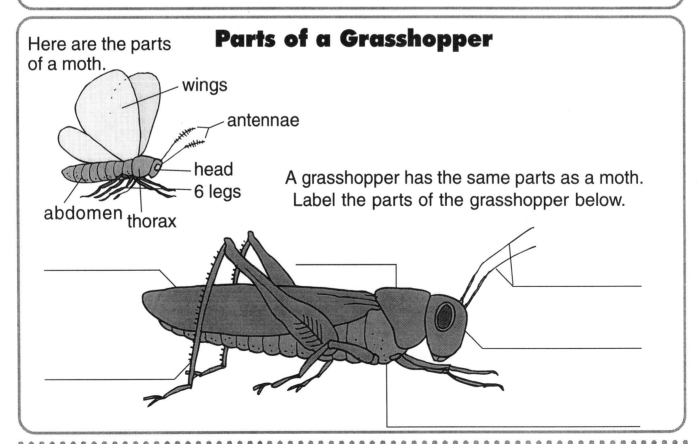

wings
antennae
head
6 legs
abdomen thorax

©1997 by Evan-Moor Corp.   26   Read and Understand Grade 3 EMC 640

Name _____

What Does It Mean?

Match each word to its meaning.

adult   the young of some insects

molt   shed skin or feathers

nymph   full-grown

female   to keep on

several   the grasshopper that lays eggs

                               more than two but not a lot

continue

Words with More Than One Meaning

Circle the correct meaning.

1. In this story **hatch** means:
   a. trap door covering
   b. come out of an egg
   c. opening in a ship's deck

2. In this story **cycle** means:
   a. a long period of time
   b. to ride a bicycle or motorcycle
   c. the steps in an insect's life

3. In this story **shed** means:
   a. to throw off old skin
   b. a building used to store things
   c. to cry tears

Name _____

Letters That Say *f*

Circle the letters that say the sound **f** in each of the following words. Draw a picture to show what the word means.

finger	calf	telephone
nymph	coffee	alphabet

Past and Present

Write the past tense of each of the following words.

lays _____laid_____   come _____

make _____   eat _____

hatch _____   molt _____

grow _____   begin _____

send _____   sleeps _____

Use the past tense words to fill in the blanks.

1. Bessie _____ me an e-mail message last night.

2. A female grasshopper _____ her eggs in the fall.

3. The nymphs _____ several times as they _____.

4. Dad and the children _____ all the pizza before mother _____ home.

5. My baby sister _____ in a cradle Grandpa _____.

Name _____

Fact or Opinion?

Put a check in the correct box to show if a sentence gives a fact or an opinion.

	fact	opinion
1. Grasshoppers eat plants.	✓	
2. Chocolate covered grasshoppers taste good.		
3. Female grasshoppers lay eggs in the ground.		
4. A nymph is a young grasshopper.		
5. Grasshoppers are pretty insects.		
6. All grasshoppers should be killed.		
7. Grasshoppers have strong legs for hopping.		

Compound Words

Circle the compound words in this paragraph. Write them on the lines below.

One morning a cowgirl was riding across a field of sunflowers. She was in a hurry to get back to the bunkhouse for breakfast. "I hope we're having pancakes with peanut butter and applesauce," she said. Just then it started to rain. Her horse Grasshopper took off in a flash. By the time they reached the ranch, the storm was over. A rainbow was sparkling in the sunshine.

cowgirl

_____   _____

_____   _____

_____   _____

_____   _____

The Three Sisters
A Native American Legend

There is a Native American story about three sisters who loved each other very much. Each sister could only be happy when she was with her sisters.

The oldest sister stood tall and golden. Her name was Corn. Corn was graceful and strong.

The middle sister liked to twine around her sister Corn. Her name was Bean. As Bean grew taller, she could give Corn a bigger hug.

The youngest sister was very brave. She stayed at the feet of Corn and Bean to protect them from danger. Her name was Squash.

Where one of the sisters grew, the other two wanted to grow. They never wanted to be separated. That is why they were always planted together in the same field.

On summer nights, when stars shine in the moonlit sky, the three sisters changed into young girls. Dressed in green, they would dance and sing. They praise their Mother Earth and their Father Sun.

Have you ever wanted a vegetable garden? Think about planting corn, bean, and squash seeds in the same mound. You will have your own "three sisters" garden. Maybe some warm summer night you'll see the three sisters dancing in the moonlight in your garden.

Name _____

Questions About *The Three Sisters*

1. Name the three sisters.

   _____

2. What does Corn look like?

   _____

3. What does Bean do?

   _____

4. What is Squash's job?

   _____

5. What happens on moonlit nights?

   _____

6. What could be true in this story?

   _____

7. What is part of the legend?

   _____

Think About It

A legend tries to explain things that happen in nature.
What did the legend of *The Three Sisters* tell us?

_____

_____

_____

Name _____

What Does It Mean?

Write the word by its meaning.

1. the first people to live in North America   _____

2. girls with the same parents   _____

3. move in a smooth and easy way   _____

4. wind around   _____

5. keep safe   _____

6. worship in song   _____

7. a hill of soil   _____

8. lighted by the moon   _____

graceful	praise
moonlit	protect
mound	sisters
Native American	twine

Write the names.

_____   _____   _____

Name_____

Spell Long e

Circle the letters that say long **e**.

see   bean   feet

fleas   clean   queen

seed   bean   please

Fill in the missing letters.

1. Did you s___ee___ the thr_____ sisters?

2. Are your hands cl_____n?

3. My dog has fl_____s.

4. Plant some b_____n s_____ds in the garden.

Add the Ending

Add **d** or **ed** to the words.
Then write sentences.

want_____   plant_____

love_____   stay_____

1. _____

2. _____

3. _____

4. _____

Name _____

Opposites

Match the opposites.

stay   youngest

oldest   hate

tall   go

love   short

summer   day

Father   winter

night   Mother

Same - Opposite

Circle words that are opposites.
Put an **X** on words that mean the same.

come - go   work - play

small - little   happy - jolly

over - under   dirty - clean

fat - thin   wet - dry

awake - asleep   sad - unhappy

late - early

Name _____

Growing a Garden

Do you have a little space for a garden? Plant the "three sisters" together. The corn will grow tall and strong. The bean vine will climb up the corn stalk. The squash will grow around the bottom of the plants. This way you can grow a lot of vegetables in a little space.

1. How can you plant corn, beans, and squash in a way that fits a small garden space?

_____

_____

2. List some of the vegetables you have eaten.

_____

_____

_____

_____

3. Now draw the vegetables you like best.

The Dog Ate My Homework

Kim woke up this morning so happy. The sun was shining. This was the Saturday she was meeting her friends to play ball at the park. Then they were going to Jiffy Burger for lunch. Then Kim remembered —she wasn't going anywhere. "Oh, no! I can't go," groaned Kim. She was on restriction. It happened this way...

Tuesday

"Where is your homework, Kim?" asked Mr. Hobbs.

"My dog ate it yesterday," said Kim.

Wednesday

"Where is your homework, Kim?" asked Mr. Hobbs.

"My baby brother ripped it up last night," said Kim.

Thursday

"Where is your homework, Kim?" asked Mr. Hobbs.

"My homework went down the kitchen drain," said Kim.

Friday

"Where is your homework, Kim?" asked Mr. Hobbs.

"I was much too sick. I needed my rest," said Kim.

That's when Mr. Hobbs called Kim's mother on the phone. The next thing Kim knew her mom was at school and Kim was in trouble— BIG trouble. She didn't even try to explain to her mom.

So now Kim is finishing up the homework lessons. And she is thinking about what she could have been doing this weekend.

Name _____

Compound Words

A compound word is made of two smaller words.

home + work = homework

Match a word in each column to make compound words.

week	noon
sun	thing
some	shine
after	end
over	water
under	sauce
apple	coat
grand	book
skate	parents
note	board

Draw pictures of these compound words.

spaceship	grasshopper
watermelon	peanut

Name _____

Base Word + Ending

Write the base word on the first line.
Write the ending on the second line.

1. hopeless   _____hope_____   _____less_____

2. slowly   _____   _____

3. playing   _____   _____

4. explains   _____   _____

5. rushes   _____   _____

6. planning   _____   _____

7. believed   _____   _____

Add an Ending

less means without   **ful** means full of
er means a person who   **ly** tells in what manner

Add the ending to make the correct word.

1. without harm   harm___less___

2. a person who teaches   teach_____

3. filled with joy   joy_____

4. in a sad way   sad_____

5. without a home   home_____

6. filled with care   care_____

7. a person who sings   sing_____

8. in a quick way   quick_____

Name _____

What Happened Next?

Pretend you are Kim from the story.
Write a letter to a friend.
Tell why you are in trouble in the order it happened.

Dear _____,

_____

_____

_____

_____

_____

_____

_____

_____

Your friend,
Kim

Off to California

Mama looked around and muttered, "Where is that child now? I told her we'd be off right after dinner time."

Mama and Pa were just about finished packing up the car. Pa was tying mattresses to the roof of the car. Mama was packing her pots and pans among the clothes and tools in the trunk. It was time to say good-by, load the children and Dog in the backseat, and hit the road. Pa wanted to get a good start before dark. They would be camping along the side of the road every night until they reached California.

Laura was hiding behind the barn. She huddled in a corner clinging to a wiggling kitten. "I won't go, Skeeter. I won't go without you. Who will take care of you if I go? It's not fair to leave you behind. Dog gets to go. Why can't you? I won't go. I won't! I won't!" she cried.

Mama looked for Laura under the porch and in the tree house. As she walked by the barn she heard Laura crying. Mama went in and sat down beside her weeping daughter.

"I know you're unhappy," said Mama as she gave Laura a hug. "But we have to go. Times are hard. There's no work around here. Uncle Henry says he can help your Pa find work if we go to his place in California."

Laura petted her kitten as she listened to Mama talk. "You know, Laura, we all have to leave behind things we love," Mama continued. "We had to sell your sister's piano and your brother's horse. And Pa and I can't take much from the house. We all will be leaving family and friends. It's hard on everyone. We just don't have a choice right now. Pa has to have work."

Laura looked up at Mama and whispered, "Will we ever get to come back home?"

Mama smiled and wiped away Laura's tears as she explained, "We're going to make a new home in California. When times are better we'll come back for a good long visit. I know it doesn't seem fair that Dog gets to go and Skeeter can't. But we're taking Dog because he is a good watch dog. There isn't much Skeeter can do to help. Don't you worry about her. Aunt Lizzie wants a kitten. She'll take good care of Skeeter."

Laura got up, hugged Mama one more time, and went to find Aunt Lizzie. She was determined to be brave and helpful as the family set off for their new home.

Name _____

Questions About *Off to California*

1. What did Mama and Pa pack in the car for the trip to California?

   _____

2. Why was the family moving to California?

   _____

3. Why was Laura hiding in the barn?

   _____

4. Mama was upset with Laura at the beginning of the story. Why was she so kind to Laura when she found her in the barn?

   _____

   _____

5. What did Mama say that made Laura feel better?

   _____

   _____

6. Why do you think they sold the piano and horse instead of leaving them with someone? _____

Think About It

Think about how you would feel if your family had to leave for a strange place with only what you could take in the car. List at least three reasons you would be unhappy.

_____

_____

Name _____

What Does It Mean?

Write each word after its meaning.

cling   determined   mutter

choice   huddle   porch

1. complain or grumble   _____

2. crowd close together   _____

3. hold tight to something   _____

4. a covered entrance to a building   _____

5. power to choose   _____

6. your mind is firmly made up   _____

More Than One Meaning

Circle the answer.

1. In the phrase "watch dog" what does **watch** mean?
   a. keep guard or protect
   b. a device for telling time
   c. to stay awake for some purpose

2. How is the word **fair** used in this story?
   a. a place to show farm produce and animals
   b. giving the same treatment to all
   c. having light-colored skin

3. What kind of **trunk** is filled in this story?
   a. an elephant's long nose
   b. the main stem of a tree
   c. a storage compartment in a car

Name _____

Word Webs

Write the correct word in each box.

Word Box			
aunt	explained	parents	trunk
backseat	Laura	roof	whispered
brother	Lizzie	sister	
cried	muttered	Skeeter	

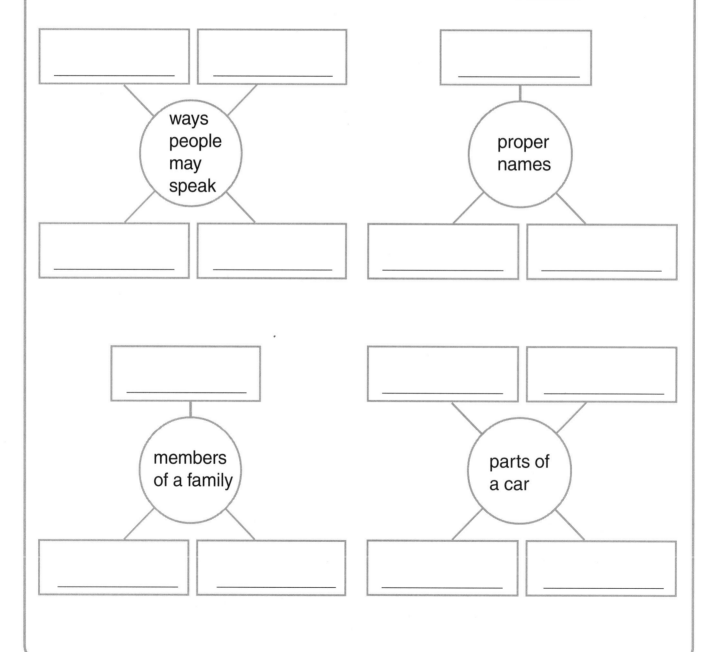

ways people may speak

proper names

members of a family

parts of a car

Name _____

Where Do You Hear *o*?

Circle the words that have the long **o** sound.

1. open
2. hello
3. flower
4. stone
5. out
6. often
7. throat

8. know
9. foam
10. of
11. joke
12. mower
13. come
14. whole

Write the long o words in the correct categories.

o - e	open syllable	oa	ow

The Sounds of *ed*

Write each word under the sound made by **ed**.

ed	d	t
headed		

headed	planned	hunted
washed	wanted	picked
begged	baked	planted
cooked	traveled	played

Name _____

Dear Diary,

This has been a crazy day. We had just started down the road this morning when we heard "thump, thump." It was a flat tire! We don't have a spare tire. Pa had to walk two miles to find a place to get it fixed. He had to use our last gas money to pay the garage man to fix it.

Pa and Mama were worrying about gas money. A farmer came by in his truck. He asked if we'd like to pick corn for him. Pa, Mama, and Sis picked corn all afternoon. They made gas cash and food money for about two days. Pa says that will get us to Uncle Henry's place in California.

While they were gone picking corn, Dog took off after a rabbit. We couldn't catch him. My brother says we can't leave the car and all our stuff to go after him. I hope he comes back when he gets hungry. That's all for now.

Good news!! A man just came by to see if we had lost a dog. It sure was good to have Dog back.

Find three problems in the story. Tell the solutions.

Problem	Solution
_____ _____	_____ _____
Problem	Solution
_____ _____	_____ _____
Problem	Solution
_____ _____	_____ _____

Harry's Helping Hand

Hi! I'm Harry. Life used to be kind of difficult for me. The muscles in my arms and legs are weak. I have to be in a wheelchair all day. I can't use my legs at all, and I'm not too great with my hands. If I drop something it stays dropped until someone picks it up for me. I can't open doors or turn lights on and off. Carrying everything I need for school is a problem too.

Now things are easier. I have a helping hand—or I should say a helping paw. Pete is a golden retriever that has been trained to help kids like me. Pete went to service dog school for two years to learn how to do dozens of different tasks. I had to be trained too. I had to learn how to give Pete commands and how to take care of him.

When Pete is working he doesn't play around. My friends know they are not to pet him or call him when he is working. He can pull my wheelchair and pick up things I drop. Pete carries my books and lunch in his backpack. He pushes the button on the school elevator and opens some kinds of doors. He even knows how to turn lights on.

But best of all, Pete is here when I need a friend.

Name _____

Questions About *Harry's Helping Hand*

1. Why did Harry need some extra help?

   _____

2. Where did Pete learn his skills?

   _____

3. Why did Harry need training?

   _____

4. How did Pete help Harry?

   _____

5. Why can't people pet Pete when he is working?

   _____

6. Who would these other service-dogs help?

   seeing-eye dog _____ hearing-ear dog _____

Think About It

Fill in the boxes with information from the story.

characters
_____   _____
problem _____
_____
_____
solution _____
_____

Name _____

What Does It Mean?

Use these words to complete the following paragraph.

taught   problems   tasks

service-dogs   wheelchair   trained

Dogs must be _____taught_____ to help blind or deaf people. The dogs go

to school for a long time to be _____. They must learn how to do

many different _____ before they are ready to be helpful. Some

_____ help people that must ride in a _____ all

day. The dogs can help solve _____ for their human partners.

Sweet is to Sugar

Write in a word to finish the comparison.

1. **hand** is to **person** as **paw** is to _____animal_____

2. **ear** is to **hear** as **eye** is to _____

3. **moon** is to **night** as **sun** is to _____

4. **bird** is to **fly** as **fish** is to _____

5. **cookie** is to **eat** as **milk** is to _____

6. **giant** is to **large** as **elf** is to _____

7. **on** is to **off** as **in** is to _____

8. **chair** is to **sit** as **bed** is to _____

Name _____

Present Tense Verbs

Add **s** or **es** to these verbs.
Use them to complete the sentences.

stay _stays_____   know _____   drop _____

push _____   open _____   take _____

pick _____   use _____   wash _____

1. Pete _stays_____ with Harry all the time.

2. Harry _____ good care of Pete.

3. Pete _____ the door for Harry.

4. He _____ how to turn on the lights.

5. Pete _____ his dish with his nose when he wants dinner.

6. Harry _____ marking pens to draw pictures.

7. He _____ Pete in the shower.

8. Pete _____ up things Harry _____.

Adding Endings

Change the **y** to **i** and add **es**.

1. carry _carries_____   5. worry _____

2. fly _____   6. study _____

3. hurry _____   7. try _____

4. cry _____   8. bury _____

Name _____

The Sounds of *oo*

Write each word under the correct sounds.

look	loose	good	soon
smooth	goose	hook	stood
balloon	shampoo	cookie	brook

b**oo**k		sch**oo**l	
look	_____	_____	_____
_____	_____	_____	_____
_____	_____	_____	_____

Opposites

Circle the words that are opposites in each sentence.

1. Tanisha closed the door Lee had opened.

2. We have to do our work before we can play.

3. Maria thinks math is easy, but science is difficult.

4. Do you know the answer to that question?

5. Lee pulled the heavy wagon while Carlos and Sam pushed it.

6. I want to learn to play checkers so I can teach my friends.

7. The train went under the tunnel before it went over the bridge.

8. Cary was so excited he was laughing and crying at the same time.

Name _____

Opposites Crossword Puzzle

Write the opposite of the clue to solve the puzzle.

Word Box

end
enemy
few
go
here
lower
noisy
question
quiet
same
something
together
wrong

Across
1. many
3. noisy
5. stay
6. nothing
7. apart
9. quiet
11. begin
12. friend

Down
2. right
3. answer
4. higher
8. there
10. different

Hush, Little Baby

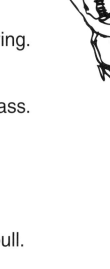

Hush, little baby, don't say a word.

Papa's going to buy you a mockingbird.

If that mockingbird won't sing,

Papa's going to buy you a diamond ring.

If that diamond ring turns brass,

Papa's going to buy you a looking glass.

If that looking glass gets broke,

Papa's going to buy you a billy goat.

If that billy goat won't pull,

Papa's going to buy you a cart and bull.

If the cart and bull turn over,

Papa's going to buy you a dog named Rover.

If the dog named Rover won't bark,

Papa's going to buy you a horse and cart.

If that horse and cart fall down,

You'll still be the sweetest little baby in town.

Name _____

Questions About *Hush, Little Baby*

1. Who is Papa singing to in this song? _____

2. Why do people sing to babies?

   _____

3. List the things Papa says he will buy:

   _____

   _____

   _____

   _____

4. What might go wrong with the following gifts?

   a. diamond ring   _____

   b. looking glass   _____

   c. cart and bull   _____

   d. Rover the dog   _____

5. What word describes the baby? _____

Think About It

Papa sang about some unusual baby gifts. What do you think a baby would really like to have?

_____

_____

Name _____

Rhyming Words

Find the word in the song that rhymes with each of the following words. Then write another word that rhymes with each pair.

1. word   _____   _____

2. glass   _____   _____

3. sing   _____   _____

4. down   _____   _____

5. pull   _____   _____

Circle the rhyming pairs. Put an X on pairs that don't rhyme.

    brass - glass   over - cover   broke - goat

    fell - bell   bark - cart   buy - fly

    you - shoe   come - home   papa - saw

Contractions

Write the long form for each of the following contractions.
Fill in the boxes to name the snack.

don't   d   o   n   o   t
                           2

you'll   ____ ____ ____   ____ ____ ____ ____ ____

won't   ____ ____ ____ ____   ____ ____ ____
                                  5

Papa's ____ ____ ____ ____   ____ ____
      1   3

can't   ____ ____ ____   ____ ____ ____
     4

isn't   ____ ____   ____ ____ ____
              7

they're ____ ____ ____ ____   ____ ____ ____
                            6

it's   ____ ____ ____   ____ ____

1	2	3	4	5	6	7
	O					

Name _____

Spell Long *i*

i-e	ie	y
mine	lie	fly

Write the word on the line.

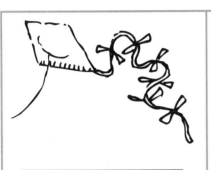

_____

_____

_____

_____

_____

_____

Compare

Use **er** to compare two things.
Use **est** to compare many things.

1. Hummingbirds are the small_____ birds.

   A robin is small_____ than an eagle.

2. Jay runs fast_____ than Pete.

   He is the fast_____ runner in class.

3. My brother is tall_____ than me.

   My dad is the tall_____ person in our family.

Name _____

What Does It Mean?

Find a word or words in the song that means the same as:

1. piece of jewelry _____

2. a sweet-singing bird _____

3. male goat _____

4. pay money for _____

5. two-wheeled vehicle _____

6. mirror _____

What Is My Name?

Write the name of each item on the line.

_____

_____

_____

_____

_____

_____

Word Box	
billy goat	baby
cart and horse	looking glass
diamond ring	mockingbird

Name _____

Good Night - Sleep Tight

Hush, Little Baby is a lullaby. Lullabies are sung to babies and young children to help them go to sleep. Write about how your parents got you to go to sleep when you were a baby.

_____

_____

_____

_____

_____

My Favorite Lullaby

Ask ten classmates to name their favorite lullaby. Complete this list.

person asked	favorite lullaby
1. _____	_____
2. _____	_____
3. _____	_____
4. _____	_____
5. _____	_____
6. _____	_____
7. _____	_____
8. _____	_____
9. _____	_____
10. _____	_____

The Fisherman and His Wife

Once upon a time long, long ago, there lived a fisherman and his wife. The couple were very poor. All they had to eat was fish the husband caught and vegetables grown by the wife. They lived in an old wooden hut by the seashore. The husband was contented going each day to fish in the sea. But his wife wanted more.

One day he caught an unusual fish. As the fisherman was looking at the fish, it began to speak. "I am an enchanted prince. Please put me back in the water before I die," said the fish. The kindhearted fisherman put it back and returned home.

"I caught a talking fish today," he told his wife. "It was really an enchanted prince." When his wife heard this she became very excited.

"Go back and call the fish. You saved its life. It should give you a reward. Tell it you want a cottage," demanded his wife.

The fisherman went back to the seashore and called, "Magic fish, I am the fisherman that put you back in the water. May I talk to you?"

When the magic fish appeared, the fisherman asked for the cottage for his wife. "Go back. She has it already," said the fish.

When he returned home, the fisherman saw a new cottage standing in place of the old hut. His wife was happy for a while, but then she began to want more. One day she said, "I am uncomfortable in this small cottage. Go back and tell the fish I want a castle. I want to be queen."

The fisherman went back to the seashore and called for the magic fish. He told the fish that his wife wanted to be queen and live in a castle. The fish said, "Return home. It is done." When he got home, he saw the castle.

His wife was happy with her castle for a while. Then she began to want more. She wanted to rule the world. Once again she sent her husband to the seashore.

When the fish appeared, the fisherman explained that now his wife was unhappy being queen. She wanted to be ruler of the world. "Return home. It is done," said the fish.

The greedy wife was happy for awhile. But she started to think about how she had no control over day and night. She called her husband and sent him to the fish again.

When the fisherman told the fish that his wife wanted to rule the moon and the sun, the magic fish became angry. "You ask for too much," shouted the magic fish. "Return to your hut." When the fisherman reached home, all he saw was their old hut. Once again the greedy wife works in her garden behind the hut. And the contented fisherman goes to the sea to catch fish for supper.

Name _____

Questions About *The Fisherman and His Wife*

1. What did the fisherman do each day?

   _____

2. What was unusual about the fish he caught?

   _____

3. Why did the wife keep sending her husband back to see the fish?

   _____

4. Why did the fish agree to grant the wife's wishes?

   _____

5. Why was the fish angry at the wife? How did he show that he was angry?

   _____

6. What word is used to describe the fisherman's wife?

   _____

7. What do you think the moral (lesson) of this story is?

   _____

Think About It

What would you ask for if you caught an enchanted fish? Why?

_____

_____

_____

_____

Name _____

The Fisherman and His Wife

Write the events in this story in the correct order.

1. _____

_____

2. _____

3. _____

4. _____

5. _____

6. _____

7. _____

8. _____

His wife wanted to rule the world.

The fisherman caught an enchanted fish.

His wife sent him to ask for a castle.

The angry fish shouted "You ask for too much!"

Once upon a time there was a poor fisherman and his wife.

His wife sent him to ask for a cottage.

The couple were back in their old hut.

His wife wanted to rule day and night.

Name _____

What Does It Mean?

Match the word to what it means in this story.

couple ———————————	a man and a woman who are married
unusual	satisfied
enchanted	came in sight
contented	under a magic spell
greedy	made the meaning clear
supper	wanting more than your share
appear	an evening meal
explain	strange or rare
rule	have control over

Draw a picture to show what this means:

cottage	castle

Name _____

Sounds of the Letter *c*

Write the sound **c** makes in these words:

cent	s	candy	k
once	_____	magic	_____
cereal	_____	city	_____
canary	_____	popcorn	_____
fence	_____	pancake	_____
cut	_____	pencil	_____

Un Means Not

The prefix **un** means not.
Add **un** to these words.
Use the new words in sentences.

un_____usual   _____comfortable   _____happy

_____

_____

_____

_____

_____

_____

_____

Name _____

Syllables

Find words in the story that have two, three, and four syllables.
Write the words here.

Two Syllables	Three Syllables	Four Syllables
_____	_____	_____
_____	_____	_____
_____	_____	
_____	_____	
_____		

Write a sentence that contains both of the four-syllable words.

_____

_____

Real and Make-Believe

List three ways you can tell this is a make-believe story.

1. _____

2. _____

3. _____

List three things in the story that could really happen.

1. _____

2. _____

3. _____

It's Not Fair!

Being the middle kid stinks! I'm always too young or too old. Mom and Dad don't listen when I say it's not fair. So I'm making a list to show them just how bad it is being in the middle.

This is my list of complaints about my big sister.

1. She stays up late watching television.
2. She goes to her friends' on school nights.
3. She gets to go places like the mall without an adult.
4. She gets a really big allowance.
5. She gets to shop for her own clothes without Mom or Dad going along.
6. She has her own computer in her room.

When I ask to do these things, my parents just say, "You're too young to do that yet."

Then there's my little brother.

1. He gets to sleep as late as he wants every morning.
2. He gets good foods like mashed potatoes while I have to eat lima beans.
3. Someone reads to him before his nap and before he goes to sleep at night.
4. He has some really great toys I never get to use.
5. We always have a baby sitter he likes when Mom and Dad go out.
6. He makes a big mess and no one complains or makes him clean it up.

When I want to do those things, my parents just say, "You're too old to do that anymore."

Being the middle kid stinks! It's not fair!

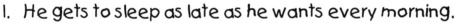

Name _____

Questions About *It's Not Fair!*

1. What was the boy in the story complaining about?

_____

_____

2. What did his parents think he was too young to do? List three things.

a. _____

b. _____

c. _____

3. What did his parents think he was too old to do? List three things.

a. _____

b. _____

c. _____

Think About It

How old do you think his big sister is? Why?

_____

_____

How old do you think his little brother is?

_____

_____

Name _____

What Does It Mean?

Color in the circle beside any correct answer.

1. What does **stinks** mean in this story?
   ○ smells bad
   ○ not fair
   ○ move slowly

2. What could you do at a **mall**.
   ○ shop for things
   ○ take a nap
   ○ find something to eat

3. What does **allowance** mean in this story?
   ○ let do something
   ○ brim on a hat
   ○ money a parent gives a child

4. What do you do if you **complain**?
   ○ tell what you want
   ○ say you don't like something
   ○ write your friend a letter

5. Which word is the opposite of **young**?
   ○ child
   ○ old
   ○ new

6. Which of these people are **adults**?
   ○ mother
   ○ father
   ○ grown-ups

Write a sentence to show you know what the word means.

(baby sitter) _____

(lima beans) _____

(fair) _____

Name _____

Silent Letters

Read the words.
Cross out the letters that don't make a sound.

lis̸ten   write   know

talk   climb   sign

Use the past tense form of the words above to fill in the blanks.

1. I _____ a letter to my friend yesterday.

2. Carlos _____ to the top of that tree.

3. We _____ to what the teacher said.

4. Tanisha _____ all the answers on the test.

Word Families

Read the clues to make the word families.

-ight

argue with someone   _____ight

not dark   _____ight

opposite of day   _____ight

we use this sense to see   _____ight

too snug   _____ight

-old

brave   _____old

opposite of hot   _____old

bend in half   _____old

spoke to someone   _____old

grows on old food   _____old

Name _____

Can You Do It?

Read the phrases at the bottom of the page.
Decide which ones someone your age can do.
Decide which ones you are still too young for.

Cut out the phrases from the story.
Paste them under the correct heading.

Too Young	I Can Do

drive a car	work in an office
fly a kite	fix my own breakfast
stay out until midnight	go to R-rated movies
stay overnight with a friend	use in-line skates
play soccer	rent an apartment

Name _____

It's Not Fair!

What would you like to do that your parents think you are too old for? Why do you think you are young enough?

_____

_____

_____

_____

_____

What would you like to do that your parents think you are too young for? Why do you think you are not too young?

_____

_____

_____

_____

_____

The Tortoise and the Hare

One fine summer day, Hare was showing off to the other animals. "I am faster than anyone in the woods," he boasted. "None of you is as quick as I am."

Slow-moving Tortoise was passing by and heard what Hare was saying. "I know someone who can beat you in a race," said Tortoise. "Me."

Hare nearly fell down laughing at the thought of such a poky animal beating him in a race. "Very well," said Hare. "I'll race you and I will win!"

The other animals marked off a race course through the woods. Tortoise and Hare came to the starting line. "Get ready. Get set. Go!" shouted Owl. Off raced Hare as fast as he could go. Soon he was so far ahead of slow-moving Tortoise that he could not see him.

"I think I'll take a little nap under this shady tree," decided Hare. "Tortoise is so far behind, he will never catch up." Soon Hare was fast asleep.

Slowly and steadily Tortoise moved along the race course. He quietly passed by the sleeping Hare and continued on his way. When Hare woke up from his nap, he couldn't see Tortoise anywhere.

"I knew that silly tortoise was the slowest animal on earth," laughed Hare as he continued the race.

Suddenly Hare heard a shout. "What is that?" he wondered. As he hurried toward the end of the race, he saw that Tortoise was only a few feet from the finish line. The loud shout he had heard was the sound of the other animals cheering for Tortoise.

Hare raced as fast as he could. There was just no way he could get to the finish line before Tortoise. The embarrassed Hare crept away as Tortoise was congratulated by his friends.

The moral of this story is: Slow and steady wins the race.

Name _____

Questions About *The Tortoise and the Hare*

1. What part did Owl take in the race between Tortoise and Hare?

   _____

2. Why did the speedy Hare lose the race?

   _____

3. Circle the words that describe the tortoise.
   Put an **X** on words that describe the hare.

quick	poky	slow-moving
steady	embarrassed	well-liked
foolish	unkind	show-off

4. What does the moral of this story mean?

   _____

   _____

Think About It

Why do you think Hare always bragged about his speed to the other animals?

_____

_____

_____

_____

_____

Name _____

What Does It Mean?

Find the words with these meanings in the story.
Write the words here.

1. a kind of turtle   _____

2. praised for winning   _____

3. uneasy and ashamed   _____

4. moved slowly   _____

5. an animal like a rabbit   _____

6. move with a regular motion _____

7. bragged   _____

Adverbs

An adverb can tell how something is done.
Fill in the missing adverbs in the following sentences.

slowly   steadily   happily   angrily

1. A tortoise moves _____ most of the time.

2. They worked _____ all day to finish the job.

3. The boy shouted _____ when the dog took his sandwich.

4. His friends cheered _____ when Tortoise won the race.

Add the suffix **ly** to the following words.
If the word ends in **y,** change the **y** to **i** and add **ly**.

happi + ly = happily

1. steady   _____   4. slow   _____

2. messy   _____   5. quick   _____

3. rapid   _____   6. angry   _____

Name _____

Long *o* Sound

Many letters make the sound of long **o**.

o   o-e   oa   ew   oe   ow

Write the name of the following long **o** pictures.

Sounds of *gh*

The letters **gh** can be pronounced like the letter **f**.
They can also be silent.
Mark what you hear in the following words.

laugh	(f)	silent	thought	f	(silent)
tough	f	silent	daughter	f	silent
night	f	silent	sleigh	f	silent
cough	f	silent	enough	f	silent
taught	f	silent	eight	f	silent

Name _____

An Interview

A reporter from the local television station is interviewing Hare and Tortoise at the scene of their big race. Write in the answers you think they would give to the reporter's questions.

Before the race:

Reporter: "Why are you racing Tortoise today?"

Hare: _____

Reporter: "How easy do you think it will be to win the race?"

Hare: _____

Reporter: "Tortoise, why do you think you can beat Hare?"

Tortoise: _____

Reporter: "What is your plan for beating Hare in the race?"

Tortoise: _____

After the race:

Reporter: "Congratulations, Tortoise. At what point did you know you would win the race?"

Tortoise: _____

Reporter: "We can't talk to Hare about the race. He seems to have disappeared."

Let's Go Snorkeling

My Aunt Gertie likes to try new things. Not only does she want to try new things, she wants you to try them, too. When you see her with a big grin on her face, you know something is about to happen. Pretty soon Aunt Gertie is saying, "Let's have an adventure."

Our last adventure together was a trip to the Hawaiian Islands. We went snorkeling to see the beautiful fish and underwater plants. But the adventure didn't start when we caught the airplane to Hawaii. We had a lot to learn before we headed to the islands.

We took snorkeling classes at the sports center. We had to learn how to breathe with a snorkel and how to dive and swim wearing a mask and fins. We learned safety tips.

Next we went to buy our equipment. We each got a snorkel, which is a tube that is used for breathing. One end goes in your mouth and the other end sticks out of the water. We bought a face mask to keep water out of our eyes and nose. And we got fins to wear on our feet. The fins help you have more power when you kick your feet as you swim.

At last we were ready to go. We packed our clothes and equipment and went to the airport. As soon as we landed, we checked in at the hotel. We changed our clothes and headed for the beach. We couldn't wait to dive in and start our underwater adventure.

Aunt Gertie is starting to grin again. What will the next adventure be?

Name _____

Questions About *Let's Go Snorkeling*

1. What makes her nephew think Aunt Gertie is so interesting?

_____

_____

2. What do you see when you go snorkeling?

_____

_____

3. What types of equipment do you need? Tell how each is used.

a. _____

b. _____

c. _____

4. Why is it important to be trained before you go snorkeling?

_____

_____

Think About It

Would you like to go snorkeling?
Give three reasons for your answer.

a. _____

b. _____

c. _____

Name _____

What Does It Mean?

Put these words from the story into the correct categories.

airport	fins	snorkel
breathe	fly	sports center
dive	Hawaiian Islands	swim
earplugs	hotel	swimsuit
face mask	kick	swimming pool

place	what you wear when snorkeling	actions
_____	_____	_____
_____	_____	_____
_____	_____	_____
_____	_____	_____
_____	_____	_____

Label this equipment:

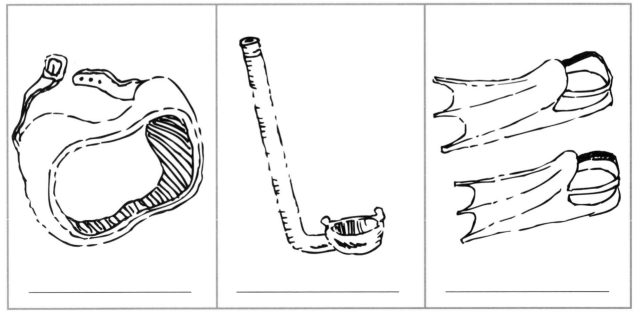

_____   _____   _____

Name _____

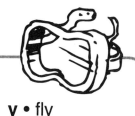

How Do You Spell Long *i*

y • dry   **i-e** • dive   **uy** • buy   **y** • fly

i • island   **igh** • high   **i** • climb

Write the missing **long i** words in this paragraph.
You will need to change two of the words.

    I took lessons to learn how to _____ into the water wearing a snor-

kel. After the lesson I _____ out of the pool to _____ off with

my towel. When my lessons were over Aunt Gertie took me to _____

snorkeling equipment. The cost of some things was very _____. Tomor-

row we are going to get on a plane and _____ to the Hawaiian

_____ for a snorkeling holiday.

More Than One

Write the plural for these words.
Use **s** or **es** for most words.
Change **y** at the end to **i** and add **es**.
A few are special plurals.

1. class   classes
2. fin   fins
3. berry   berries
4. man   men
5. book   _____
6. dish   _____
7. baby   _____

8. island   _____
9. beach   _____
10. woman   _____
11. bunny   _____
12. jet   _____
13. child   _____
14. house   _____
15. goose   _____
16. story   _____

Name _____

What Happened Next?

Cut and paste in order.

1.

2.

3.

4.

5.

6.

We took classes to learn to use the equipment.

Aunt Gertie said, "Let's have an adventure."

We saw fish and plants under the water.

Aunt Gertie and I flew to the Hawaiian Islands.

We bought our own snorkeling equipment.

Aunt Gertie is grinning again. What will her next adventure be?

Name _____

Find the Answers

You want to learn how to snorkel. Read the advertisement below and then follow these directions.

1. Circle in red the words that tell how much the lessons cost.
2. Put a blue box around the place you have to go.
3. Underline in green the day of the week the lesson are given.
   Put two green lines under the time of day.
4. Are you old enough to take the lessons?
   Yes   No

> **Learn to Snorkel**
> Markham Sports Center
> Saturday 8:00 - 10:00 A.M.
> 6 lessons only $50
> Must be 8 years or older.

Snorkeling Adventure Wordsearch

```
A D V E N T U R E X E S
H V W S N O R K E L Q P
A I R P O R T I M I U O
W G O O S W I M P S I R
A F T R D I V E L L P T
I F I T S A F E A A M I
I Z I S M A S K N N E N
F U N N H F L Y T D N W
U N D E R W A T E R T E
L E A R N Q H O T E L T
```

Find these words.

✓ adventure	_____ fish	_____ island	_____ snorkel
_____ airport	_____ fly	_____ learn	_____ sport
_____ dive	_____ fun	_____ mask	_____ swim
_____ equipment	_____ Hawaii	_____ plant	_____ trip
_____ fin	_____ hotel	_____ safe	_____ underwater
			_____ wet

Alligators and Crocodiles

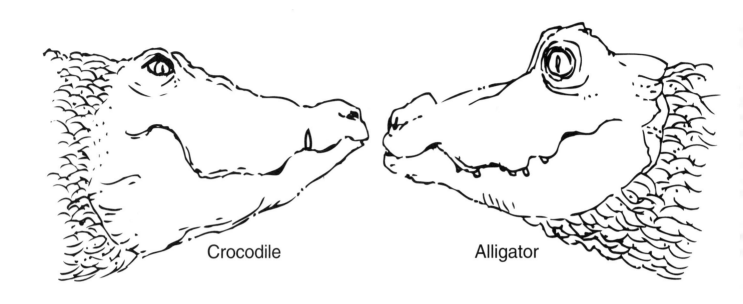

Crocodile   Alligator

Alligators and crocodiles are reptiles. Like other reptiles, they have dry, scaly skin and lay eggs. They are cold-blooded. This means they can't make heat to keep their bodies warm on a cold day. They have to be in a warm place to stay warm. That is why they are found most often in hot climates.

When these reptiles lie still, their greenish-brown bodies look like big logs. This can trick other animals into coming so close they become dinner!

Most crocodiles and alligators live near fresh water. A few, like the saltwater crocodile, live in places where rivers flow into the sea and the water is salty.

Their bodies have adapted to life in the water. Eyes and nostrils are set on top of their heads. They can see and breathe when the rest of the body is underwater. The nostrils close to keep out water. A transparent flap of skin covers the eye so it can see under water.

An alligator has a round, wide snout. A crocodile's snout is narrower. A lower tooth on each side shows when a crocodile closes it mouth. It doesn't show on an alligator.

Both crocodiles and alligators are hunters. They feed on large animals like cattle and smaller animals like birds and fish. They use their powerful tails, sharp teeth, and strong jaws to capture food. Their teeth are not good for tearing or chewing food. They shake their prey around to tear off big chunks which are then swallowed whole. Teeth are often lost, but new teeth quickly replace them. They may grow fifty or more sets of teeth in a lifetime.

In the water these reptiles swim by moving their tails. On land, crocodiles move quickly with their front and back legs working together. Alligators usually slither along on their stomachs with their legs spread out at their sides.

Crocodiles dig nests in the sand for their eggs. They lay the eggs and cover them up. Alligators make a pile of plant material, lay their eggs, and cover them up with more plant material. When the eggs are ready to hatch, the babies begin to make noises in their shells. The mothers uncover the nests. The hatchlings head for water as soon as they leave the nest. Alligators and some crocodiles help their babies to water by carrying them in their mouths or on their backs.

The hatchlings eat small worms, snails, and insects. Even though the mothers look after their young while they are small, many are eaten by other animals before they are grown.

Name _____

Questions About *Alligators and Crocodiles*

1. Describe a reptile.

_____

_____

2. Why do reptiles need to live where it is warm?

_____

_____

3. List three ways crocodiles and alligators are suited for life in the water.

   a._____

   b._____

   c._____

4. What is unusual about the teeth of crocodiles and alligators?

_____

5. How do crocodiles and alligators know when their eggs are ready to hatch?

_____

6. Label the pictures:

_____   _____

Think About It

Why is it a bad idea to sell baby alligators and crocodiles as pets?

_____

_____

Name _____

What Does It Mean?

Color the circle in front of the correct meaning.

1. Which word tells what is on the outside of a **reptile**?
   ○ fur
   ○ scales
   ○ feathers

2. Which phrase means **prey**?
   ○ animals caught for food
   ○ to say grace
   ○ scaly animals

3. Crocodiles and alligators live in hot regions. Which two words mean the same as **region**?
   ○ a place
   ○ a swamp
   ○ an area

4. Mark the scaly **reptiles** listed below.
   ○ snake
   ○ alligator
   ○ turtle

5. Mark the word from this story that means an animal **just out of its egg**.
   ○ young
   ○ hatchling
   ○ calf

6. What words from the story mean the opposite of **fresh water**?
   ○ used water
   ○ new water
   ○ salty water

Use clues in the story to help you write the meaning of the following words.

1. transparent _____

2. cold-blooded _____

Name _____

What Says *er*?

Circle the letters that say **er** in each of these words.

w(or)d   bird   turn   her   early

Use the letters you circled to fill in the missing letters:

My moth__er__ is a n_____se. H_____ w_____k is very important. Last

Friday aft_____noon she left w_____k _____ly so we could go to the movies

togeth_____. But f_____st we ate at the pizza parl_____ next to the movie

theat_____.

The movie was about a gigantic monst_____ cov_____ed in f_____. The

monst_____ went around the _____th frightening everyone.

Articles

The articles **a** and **an** come before a noun.
A is used before words starting with a consonant sound.
An is used before words starting with a vowel sound.

_____ alligator   _____ crocodile   _____ egg

_____ nest   _____ tooth   _____ pony

_____ angel   _____ snout   _____ orange

_____ tail   _____ insect   _____ octopus

Name _____

Antonyms

Write words that mean the opposite of the following words.

1. soft _____

2. angry _____

3. huge _____

4. rapid _____

5. day _____

6. dangerous _____

7. chilly _____

8. empty _____

9. heavy _____

10. awake _____

11. raw _____

12. dirty _____

asleep	full	light	slow
clean	hard	night	small
cooked	happy	safe	warm

What Doesn't Belong

Cross out the word that does not belong.

eyes	alligator	pond
mouth	turtle	river
~~toes~~	snake	creek
nostrils	bird	stream

capture	hat	chair
release	bonnet	bench
trap	cap	table
catch	ribbon	stool

Name _____

Crocodile and Alligator

Fill in the chart to show the differences between a crocodile and an alligator.

	Crocodile	Alligator
movement on land		
snout shape		
teeth position		
nest material and location		

Daedalus and Icarus

A Greek Myth

Daedalus was an architect and an inventor. Minos, the king of the island of Crete, hired Daedalus to design his palace. King Minos became angry with Daedalus when he helped one of the king's enemies escape. The king locked Daedalus and his son in a tower and wouldn't let them leave Crete.

"There is no escape by land, and Minos controls the sea. But he does not control the air. That is how we will escape!" Daedalus told his son.

Icarus gathered feathers of the gulls that soared over the island, while Daedalus designed a pair of wings. He made a wooden frame and attached the gull feathers with wax and string. He studied the flight of the island birds to learn how they moved their wings to rise in the sky. He watched to see how they hovered on the air currents.

Pronunciation Key	
Daedalus	ded' l us
Icarus	ik' u rus
Minos	mi' nus
Sicily	sis' u lee

When the wings were ready, Daedalus called Icarus to him. He said, "My son, what we are about to do is very dangerous. Listen carefully to what I say. Keep to the middle path between heaven and earth. Do not go too near the sun for its heat will melt the wax. Do not go too near the sea. The fog will wet the feathers and the wings will become too heavy. Stay close to me and no harm will come to you."

At first Icarus followed his father as he had been told. But soon he couldn't resist the temptation to fly higher. Ignoring his father's cry of warning, Icarus flew higher and higher.

When he felt the warm wax running over his shoulders, Icarus realized his mistake. He tried to flutter his wings, but no feathers remained. Icarus fell from the sky, plunged into the sea, and drowned.

Daedalus hurried to save the boy, but he was too late. He picked up Icarus in his arms and flew to land. After Daedalus buried Icarus, he flew to the island of Sicily. There he remained for the rest of his life.

Name _____

Questions About *Daedalus and Icarus*

1. Why did Daedalus and Icarus have to escape from Minos by air?

_____

2. What were the wings made of?

_____

3. Why did Daedalus need to observe flying birds?

_____

4. Why did Icarus's wings fall apart?

_____

5. Why should Icarus have listened to his father's instructions?

_____

6. What two islands are named in the story?

_____

Think About It

Think of a time when you didn't listen to a warning or instruction. What happened?

_____

_____

_____

_____

Name _____

What Does It Mean?

Match the word to its meaning.

inventor   fall

soared   rose up in the air

design   creator of new things

temptation   injure or damage

warning   make a plan

ignore   to not pay attention

plunge   something that draws you to it

harm   notice of danger

Too - To - Two

Fill in the blanks.

1. Juan planned a trip _____ the aquarium.

2. Alan needs _____ new tires for his bike.

3. Kelly wants new tires _____.

Write a sentence with each word.

(to) _____

(too) _____

(two) _____

Name _____

The Sounds of *ou*

Listen to the vowel sound in each word. Write the symbols to show the sound.

ow - loud	ō - though
ŏŏ - could	ōō - your
aw - thought	u - country

1. should   _____ŏŏ_____

2. shoulder   _____ō_____

3. cloud _____

4. cousin _____

5. you _____

6. bought _____

7. hour _____

8. boulder _____

9. about _____

10. couple _____

11. ouch _____

12. cough _____

13. would _____

14. court _____

15. tour _____

16. enough _____

Synonyms

Match the words that mean about the same thing.

design   collect

angry   mad

gather   injure

dangerous   happiness

middle   plan

near   caution

harm   fall

joy   stay

warn   center

remain   unsafe

plunge   close

Name _____

Add a Suffix

Write each base word with a suffix.

1. Drop the **e** and add the endings **ing** and **ed**.

move _____ _____

hope _____ _____

smile _____ _____

Just add the ending **s**.

move _____

hope _____

smile _____

2. Double the last letter and add the ending **ed** and **ing**.

hop _____ _____

control _____ _____

plan _____ _____

Just add the ending **s**.

hop _____

control _____

plan _____

3. Change **y** to **i** and add the ending **s** and **ed**

hurry _____ _____

study _____ _____

bury _____ _____

Just add the ending **ing**.

hurry _____

study _____

bury _____

Name _____

Cause and Effect

Write the effect of the causes listed below.

Cause	Effect
The king was angry and would not let Daedalus leave the island.	_____ _____ _____
Daedalus observed how birds flew.	_____ _____ _____
Icarus ignored his father's warning about flying too near the sun.	_____ _____ _____

Draw What Happened

Daedalus building wings.	Icarus flying too near the sun.

When Granny Met Johnny Appleseed

"Tell us a story, Granny," begged the children, for Granny was the best storyteller in the whole state. She was very, very old and had lived in many places, experienced many adventures, and known many interesting people.

"Well, you youngin's have been mighty good all day. I guess I can remember one story," said Granny. "Did I ever tell you about the time I met Johnny Appleseed?"

"You met Johnny Appleseed?" asked the children.

"Yep. I was just a little mite when Ma, Pa, and me headed west," answered Granny...

It was a long, hard trip travelin' by covered wagon. When we stopped, Pa would collect firewood and Ma would start supper. While Pa took care of the oxen and Ma cooked, I was supposed to stay out of the way.

Well, one evening, while I was stayin' out of the way, I spied a little rabbit. It was as cute as a button. I started followin' it, and the next thing I knew I was lost in the woods. I started to blubber and tears fell down my cheeks. Then I started to bawl big, loud sobs.

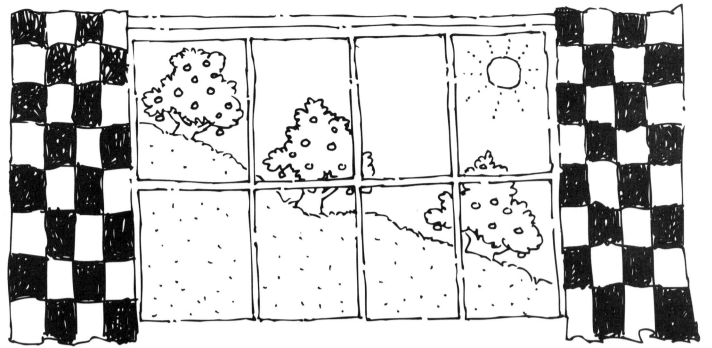

"My, my, what's the matter youngin'? Why are you raisin' such a ruckus?" asked a funny-looking old man. "Are you lost?" I whispered, "Yes." He said, "Now don't you be scared. I'll take you back to your folks."

I'd never seen anyone that looked so strange. He was dressed in worn out old clothes, his feet were bare, and he had on a funny hat. But I wasn't afraid. He had a kind smile and a twinkle in his eyes.

"Folks call me Johnny Appleseed," he said after Ma and Pa thanked him for finding me. Ma invited Johnny to eat with us. While we ate he told us about how he was travelin' west with his apple seeds. Everywhere he stopped, he planted apple seeds and made friends. He was friendly with the Indians, the settlers, and the wild animals in the woods.

After supper Johnny gave me a handful of apple seeds. "Plant these seeds when you settle, youngin'," he said. Then he disappeared into the woods.

"Did you plant the seeds, Granny?" asked the children.

"Yep," said Granny. "Look out the window and you can see them growin' on the side of the hill. And I've got me a hankerin' right now to pick some and make an apple pie for supper."

Name _____

Questions About *Granny and Johnny Appleseed*

1. Why did Granny agree to tell the children a story?

_____

2. Where was Granny's family headed?

_____

3. How did she get lost?

_____

4. Describe the man who found her.

_____

5. Why wasn't she afraid of the strange man?

_____

6. How did Johnny Appleseed get his nickname?

_____

_____

7. Where did the apple trees on the hillside come from?

_____

8. Granny planned to make an apple pie for supper. What are some other ways she could have used the apples?

_____

Think About It

Do you think it is possible that Granny really met Johnny Appleseed? Why or why not?

_____

_____

_____

Name _____

Add *ing*

In this story the **g** was dropped at the end of words with an **ing** ending. This is the way many people spoke in earlier times. Some people still speak this way today in everyday speech.

Correct the spelling of these words in the following sentences.

1. We were travelin' west in a covered wagon.   _traveling_

2. I was stayin' out of the way while Ma cooked.   _____

3. The bear cub was followin' its mother.   _____

4. Granny is raisin' apples on the hillside.   _____

5. She was wishin' for a pet of her very own.   _____

6. They were goin' for a walk in the park.   _____

Similes

The rabbit in the story *When Granny Met Johnny Appleseed* is called "as cute as a button." This type of figure of speech is called a simile. Similes compare two things in interesting or funny ways.

Match the parts of the following similes.

as cute	as a mule
as mad	as a button
as stubborn	as an owl
as wise	as a penny
as strong	as a bug in a rug
as bright	as a wet hen
as snug	as an ox

Write your own similes.

1. as happy as   _____

2. as big as   _____

3. as cool as   _____

4. as fast as   _____

5. as old as   _____

Name _____

What Does It Mean?

Color in the circle to tell what each word means.

1. The word **youngin'** means:
   ○ a child
   ○ a baby animal
   ○ a small baby

2. When you **blubber**, you are:
   ○ making bubbles
   ○ taking a bath
   ○ crying

3. If you answer **yep** you are saying:
   ○ no
   ○ yes
   ○ maybe

4. A **ruckus** is a:
   ○ fight
   ○ noisy commotion
   ○ kind of backpack

5. If you have a **hankerin'** you:
   ○ want to do or have something
   ○ need a handkerchief
   ○ have a headache

6. In this story the word **folks** was used for:
   ○ Granny and the children
   ○ Ma and Pa
   ○ people Johnny met

7. In this story **mighty** was used to mean:
   ○ strong
   ○ big
   ○ very

8. Johnny Appleseed was a **nickname**. Do you have a nickname? What is it? How did you get this nickname? Who gave it to you?

   _____

   _____

Name _____

Spelling Long *a*

Circle the correct spelling.

1. _____ your hand if you have a question. (raise) raze

2. Mother set the flowers on the _____. tayble table

3. Mario is the best _____ in our league. plaier player

4. My grandparents flew here on a jet _____. plain plane

5. Don't be _____ to try new things. afrayed afraid

6. The astronaut flew into outer _____. space spaice

7. Kelly broke the white _____ in her box. craion crayon

8. Mr. Lee was elected _____ of the city. mayor mare

Pronouns

she	he	I	we	they	it
her	him	me	us	them	

Replace the underlined noun with a pronoun.

1. <u>Granny</u> is a great storyteller. _____ She _____

2. Ma invited <u>Johnny</u> to eat supper. _____

3. The girl followed <u>the rabbit</u>. _____

4. <u>Ma and Pa</u> worked hard. _____

5. Granny picked <u>apples</u> for a pie. _____

6. <u>Johnny</u> gave the girl apple seeds. _____

7. <u>Ma and I</u> like apple pie. _____

8. Granny made pie for <u>the children</u>. _____

Name _____

Who Was Johnny Appleseed?

Go to the library to find out more about the real man that was called Johnny Appleseed. Write a paragraph about what you learn.

I read _____.

(title of book, magazine, or encyclopedia)

This is what I learned:

Draw Johnny Appleseed.

Koala

The koala is a mammal that lives in Australia. It has thick fur to keep it warm and dry. Its baby is born live and is fed milk from the mother's body. In all of these ways a koala is like other mammals. But a koala is a special kind of mammal called a marsupial. A female marsupial has a pouch on her underside. This is where she carries her baby as it grows.

When a koala baby is born, it is blind and has no hair. The baby is only about the size of a lima bean. This tiny baby must crawl up into its mother's pouch. There it will eat, sleep, and grow. Even after it is able to come out of the pouch, it will hop back in when it is scared or sleepy. The baby koala rides on its mother's back until it can take care of itself.

A koala eats the leaves of eucalyptus (gum) trees. It eats the tender shoots that grow on the tips of the branches. A koala has two sharp teeth in front for tearing leaves or stripping bark. It has flat teeth in back for chewing the leaves. A koala may go on the ground to move to a new tree.

A koala does sometimes drink, but the leaves it eats provide most of the water it needs.

The koala is a nocturnal animal. This means it is more active at night than during the day. A koala doesn't have a home or a nest. It just wedges its body into the fork of a tree. It wraps its arms or legs around a branch, closes its eyes, and goes to sleep.

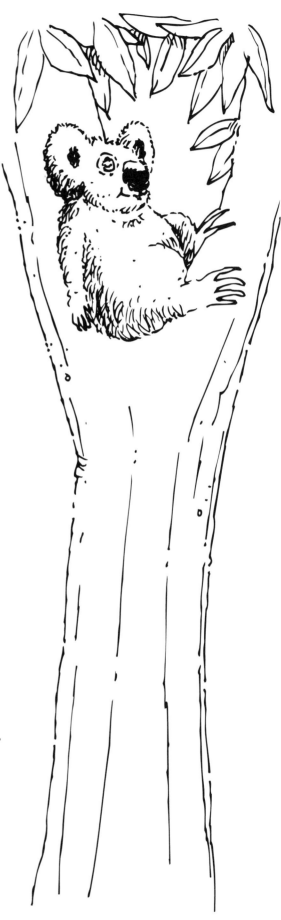

Name _____

Questions About *Koala*

1. How is a koala the same as other mammals?

   _____

2. How is a koala different than other mammals?

   _____

3. Describe how a koala uses its teeth to eat.

   _____

   _____

4. How does a koala sleep if it doesn't have a nest or burrow?

   _____

   _____

5. Why doesn't a male koala have a pouch?

   _____

Think About It

Marsupials

koala
- two thumbs on each hand for climbing
- eats eucalyptus leaves
- found in Australia

wombat
- sharp claws for digging burrows
- eats grass
- found in Australia

kangaroo
- large feet for hopping
- eats grass and low-growing plants
- found in Australia

Write a general statement about the three animals on the chart.

_____

_____

_____

_____

_____

_____

Name _____

What Does It Mean?

Use the correct word in each sentence.

nocturnal   marsupials   mammal   eucalyptus

wedge   female   pouch   Australia

1. A ___mammal___ mother feeds her baby milk.

2. Only the _____ koala has babies.

3. At night _____ animals become active.

4. A koala baby grows up in its mother's _____.

5. Koalas _____ themselves in a fork of a tree to sleep.

6. Animals with pouches are called _____.

7. The _____ is a kind of tree.

8. Most marsupials live in _____.

Words With More Than One Meaning

Circle the correct meaning.

1. In this story **gum** means:

something to chew   a eucalyptus tree

2. In this story **fork** means:

where two branches come together   a tool we eat with

3. In this story **bark** means:

the outside layer of a tree   the sound a dog makes

4. In this story **shoots** means:

fires a gun   tender new growth on a tree

Name _____

Words Into Syllables

A VCCV word is divided into syllables between the two consonants.

| funnel | fun - nel |
| circus | cir - cus |

Divide the following words.

1. funny   _fun_ - _ny_   5. only   _____ - _____

2. tender   _____ - _____   6. into   _____ - _____

3. pencil   _____ - _____   7. monster   _____ - _____

4. basket   _____ - _____   8. candle   _____ - _____

Who Owns It?

only one owner - add **'s**
mother's purse

more than one owner - add **s'**
two birds' nest

irregular plural - add **'s**
children's lunches

exception to the rule - **its**
its saddle

Circle the missing word.

1. Put the letter on _____ table.   mother's   mothers'

2. The baby koala is in _____ pouch.   it's   its

3. All the _____ bikes were blue.   boy's   boys'

4. The _____ cars were in a wreck.   men's   mens'

5. My horse ate all _____ oats.   its'   its

6. A dog ate the _____ lunches.   childrens   children's

Rewrite each phrase using an apostrophe.

1. pouch of a koala baby   _koala baby's pouch_

2. letter for Mario   _____

3. cookies for the children   _____

4. new leash for it   _____

5. ship for the captain   _____

6. toys belonging to the kittens   _____

Name _____

Compare Life Cycles

Think about how a koala and a dog are alike and how they are different. Mark the chart below to show this.

	Koala	Dog	Both
1. The baby is fed mother's milk.			
2. The baby grows inside mother until birth.			
3. The mother protects the baby.			
4. The baby is born live.			
5. The baby is born before it is fully formed.			
6. The baby's body is covered with hair.			
7. The baby is the size of a lima bean when born.			
8. The mother has many babies at one time.			

What Koalas Can Do - A Word Search

Circle the verbs in this list.
Then find them in the word search.

born	grow	carry
tear	tree	crawl
koala	eat	strip
feed	chew	wedge
slow	sleep	wrap
go	see	walk
pouch	climb	drink

```
C L I M B W R A P S W
R E S L E E P G D C A
A C A R R Y X O R H L
W H S T R I P Z I O K
L E S E E B O R N O W
Q W E D G E F X K L Y
T E A R G Z F F E E D
```

Name _____

Koala Crossword Puzzle

Word Box

Australia
bark
eucalyptus
gum
koala
lima
mammal
marsupial
nocturnal
pouch
shoots
tree

Across

1. an animal that feeds milk to its young
4. the country where koalas are native
5. the outside covering of a tree
7. koalas eat the leaves of this tree
11. the name for animals that are active after dark

Down

1. a mammal with a pouch
2. where a koala eats and sleeps
3. a newborn koala is the size of a ___ bean
6. another name for the eucalyptus tree
8. new growth on the tips of tree branches
9. a kind of marsupial
10. where a marsupial carries her baby

Shannon Lucid - Astronaut

How would you feel if your mom was away in outer space? That's what happened to the children of astronaut Shannon Lucid. She spent 188 days on the Russian space station Mir (meer). She and two Russian cosmonauts made over 3,000 trips around the earth. She sent e-mail to her family every day. Her favorite snack, M&Ms, was sent up to her in space capsules.

Mrs. Lucid was born in Shanghai, China, where her parents were missionaries. In 1949, the family settled in Oklahoma, where Shannon grew up. Since childhood she had wanted to explore space. She learned to fly a plane, and she studied science in college. These skills helped her become one of the first group of women astronauts.

Being weightless for a long time can make bones brittle and muscles weak. After a long time in space, astronauts are weak for a while. Some have to be carried off the shuttle. Lucid's project on the Mir was to exercise. She exercised for a couple of hours every day. Doctors wanted to see if this would help keep her body strong. She was wobbly, but able to walk off the shuttle. Lucid will have check-ups over the next few years. Doctors want to see if there are any long-term changes in her bones and muscles from her time in space.

And what does Shannon Lucid want to do next? She says she'd like to go to Mars.

Name _____

Questions About *Shannon Lucid*

1. What is Mir? _____

2. Who was on board Mir with Shannon Lucid?

    _____

3. What does the story tell you about Shannon Lucid's childhood?

    _____

4. What did she study that helped her become an astronaut?

    _____

5. How did she keep in touch with her family while out in space?

    _____

6. What was her project on the space station?

    _____

7. Do you think she enjoyed her trip in space? Why?

    _____

Think About It

What questions would you ask Shannon Lucid if you met her?

_____

_____

Would you like to be an astronaut someday? Give at least two reasons for your answer.

_____

_____

_____

Name _____

What Does It Mean?

Write the word by its meaning in this story.

1. the Russian space station   _____

2. an American space traveler   _____

3. a city in China   _____

4. having no weight   _____

5. a Russian space traveler   _____

6. use your body to get stronger   _____

7. shaky; unsteady   _____

8. manned satellite orbiting the earth   _____

9. a person sent by a church to   _____
   teach religious ideas and to help people

astronaut	Mir	space station
cosmonaut	missionary	weightless
exercise	Shanghai	wobbly

What Happened Next?

Complete the sentences to tell events in Shannon Lucid's life.

1. Shannon Lucid was born _____.

2. She grew up in _____.

3. She learned how to _____.

4. She studied _____.

5. She was one of the first _____.

6. She spent 188 days _____.

7. Next she would like to _____.

Name _____

Space Adventure

Circle the verbs in the story.
Write them in the correct boxes below.

The spaceship blasted off early yesterday morning. Alex felt excited and worried at the same time. He looked out the window as the Earth grew smaller and smaller.

The trip to Zennox took three months. Alex exercised every day. He wanted to be strong when he reached the distant planet. At last he arrived.

"What happens first?" muttered Alex.

He read his schedule of procedures.

> 1. Put on spacesuit and pack equipment.
> 2. Examine shuttle to see that everything still works.
> 3. Fly to the surface.
> 4. Collect rock samples.
> 5. Return to ship.

Alex climbed into the shuttle. He smiled as he started the engine. He took off for the new planet.

Present Tense	Past Tense

©1997 by Evan-Moor Corp.   116

Name _____

Dreams

Shannon Lucid dreamed of becoming a space explorer when she grew up. What do you dream of becoming? Why do you want to do this?

_____

_____

_____

_____

_____

Mrs. Lucid learned to fly a plane and studied science. These helped her become an astronaut. What could you learn that will help you reach your dream?

_____

_____

_____

_____

_____

Name _____

Before - After

A prefix comes in front of a word to change it.

    pre - before   **un** - not

A suffix comes at the end of a word to change it.

    less - without   **ful** - filled with

Add a prefix or suffix to the words.

1. not able to   _____able   5. not happy   _____happy

2. filled with joy   joy_____   6. see before   _____view

3. no weight   weight_____   7. very pretty   beauti_____

4. before the game _____game   8. no money   penni_____

Now write a sentence with each of the new words you made.

1. _____

2. _____

3. _____

4. _____

5. _____

6. _____

7. _____

8. _____

Vampire Bats

Eli saw a really scary movie on television last night. In the movie a man turned into a vampire and attacked people to drink their blood. Eli woke up in the middle of the night screaming "No! No! Don't suck my blood!" His father decided it was time to visit the library and find out the truth about vampires. This is what Eli learned.

There really are vampire bats. But they are not like the vampires you see in the movies. And although these small bats drink blood, they don't usually bite humans.

Vampire bats live in the warm tropical parts of Central and South America. They sleep during the day and come out at night to feed on blood of other animals.

The hungry vampire lands near a sleeping animal. It climbs onto its prey to feed. With razor-sharp teeth, the vampire bat makes a small incision on a bare part of the animal. A vampire bat has something in its saliva that keeps this blood from clotting. The blood stays thin as the vampire eats. The vampire doesn't suck the blood up through fangs. It laps the blood up like a kitten laps up milk.

There is one way a vampire bat can be harmful. Many of these little bats carry serious diseases, including rabies. As they eat they can give these diseases to other animals.

Eli learned two important things. One—people don't turn into blood-sucking vampires. And two—don't watch scary movies before going to bed. They can give you nightmares!

Name _____

Questions About *Vampire Bats*

1. What caused Eli to have a nightmare?

   _____

2. List five true things Eli learned about vampire bats.

   a. _____

   b. _____

   c. _____

   d. _____

   e. _____

3. Why is it dangerous to handle wild animals, even small ones like a vampire bat? _____

4. What do you think a person should do if bitten by a bat?

   _____

Think About It

Eli had a nightmare after watching a scary movie. Write about a nightmare you have had and tell what you think caused it.

_____

_____

_____

_____

Name _____

Spelling Long Vowel Sounds

Write the long vowel sound you hear.
Circle the letter or letter combination that spells the sound.

1. they   _____ā_____

2. time   _____

3. scream _____

4. night   _____

5. go   _____

6. sleep   _____

7. day   _____

8. though _____ō_____

9. movie   _____

10. cute   _____

11. cloak _____

12. fly   _____

13. human _____

14. strain _____

List all the ways these sounds were spelled.

long a	long e	long o	long i	long u
_____	_____	_____	_____	_____
_____	_____	_____	_____	_____
_____	_____	_____	_____	_____

Y at the End

Read the following list of words.
Write the sound of the letter y.

1. scary   _____e_____

2. fly   _____

3. carry   _____

4. happy   _____

5. my   _____

6. try   _____

At the end of many one-syllable words **y** says _____.

At the end of many two-syllable words **y** says _____.

Name _____

What Does It Mean?

Complete the crossword puzzle.

Word Box

bat
bare
blood
clot
decide
fang
incision
nightmare
rabies
saliva
serious
vampire

Across

3. a liquid in the mouth; spit
6. a frightening dream
8. not covered
9. a cut
10. important; needing thought
11. when blood thickens after a cut

Down

1. a blood-eating bat
2. a flying mammal
4. a disease of warm-blooded animals
5. to make up your mind
7. a long, sharp tooth
8. a red fluid in the body

Name _____

True - False

Write true or false after each statement.

1. Vampire bats eat blood. _____ true _____

2. People can turn into vampires. _____

3. You can learn about vampires at the library. _____

4. Vampires suck up blood with their fangs. _____

5. Vampire bats can carry diseases. _____

6. Vampires have razor-sharp teeth. _____

7. Vampire bats eat during the day and
   sleep when it is dark. _____

8. A vampire's saliva makes blood stay thin
   so it is easier to eat. _____

9. Vampire bats live all over the world. _____

Illustrate:

a true vampire	a vampire in a nightmare

Name _____

Alike and Different

Think of what you know about birds and about the vampire bat.
How are they alike and how are they different?
Put at least three facts in each space on this diagram.

birds only

both birds and vampire bats

vampire bats only

George Washington Carver

If someone asked "What can you make out of peanuts?" what would you answer? Most of us would think of peanut butter or peanut cookies. One man didn't stop thinking up new ways until he had thought of more than 100.

George Washington Carver was born in 1864. He was born a slave. When he was still a baby, his mother was stolen. He and his brother were kept by his master, Moses Carver, and his wife, Susan.

All his life George loved plants. When he was only seven years old, he already knew so much about plants people in his home town called him "the plant doctor."

George wanted to learn as much as he could, but there was no school for black children where he lived. When he was ten, he left home to find a town that would allow black children to attend school. He went to schools in Missouri and Kansas until he finished high school. All this time he had to work to pay his own expenses. He worked as a cook and opened his own laundry.

In 1890, George began college. At first he studied art, but he still had a love of plants. He began to study agriculture. After he graduated, the famous inventor Thomas Edison asked him to come to work in his laboratory. George turned him down. He had other plans. He started an agricultural department at Tuskegee Normal School, a new university for black students in Alabama.

In those days, many farmers in the south grew only cotton. This was hard on the soil. After a while the cotton would not grow as well. George Washington Carver wanted to help farmers in the south to grow plants like peanuts and sweet potatoes. These plants helped the soil. Over the years he invented hundreds of ways to use these two plants.

George Washington Carver invented so many things he was called "The Wizard of Tuskegee." He died in 1943 at the age of 79.

Name _____

Questions About *George Washington Carver*

1. Why was George raised by Moses and Susan Carver?

   _____

2. What did George do at...

   seven years old?   _____

   ten years old?   _____

   in 1890?   _____

3. Who wanted Mr. Carver to work in his laboratory after he graduated from college? Why did he say no? _____

   _____

4. How did Mr. Carver help southern farmers?

   _____

   _____

5. What did he do for Tuskegee Normal School?

   _____

6. How did Mr. Carver earn the nickname "The Wizard of Tuskegee"?

   _____

7. List the three states named in the story.

   _____

Think About It

It was difficult for George Washington Carver to go to school when he was a boy. How would it be different for him if he lived now?

_____

_____

Name _____

What Does It Mean?

Word Box

agriculture
invent
laundry
master
peanut
slave
sweet potato
university
wizard

Across

5. farming
8. create something new
9. a place where clothes
   are washed and ironed

Down

1. seed of one kind of plant
2. where you go to learn
   after high school
3. a type of vegetable
4. a person owned by someone else
6. a person who owns slaves
7. a very clever person

Name _____

Sounds of *ow*

Read the words.
Put them in the right boxes.

ow	$\bar{o}$
_____	_____
_____	_____
_____	_____
_____	_____

allow	crowd	own
blow	flow	sown
brow	flower	tow
		town

In the Past

Write the past for each word.
Then fill in the blanks in the sentences.

run <u>ran</u>   grow _____

keep _____   find _____

begin _____   blow _____

1. Many slaves _____ away from their masters.

2. He _____ his car in the garage.

3. The flowers _____ to bloom in the spring.

4. The farmer _____ peanuts and sweet potatoes.

5. The children _____ hidden treasure in the cave.

6. Toby _____ out the candles on his birthday cake.

Name _____

Peanuts

List all of the ways you have eaten peanuts or seen peanuts used.

_____

_____

_____

_____

Made From Peanuts

Find some of the products that George Washington Carver made from peanuts in this wordsearch.

axle	grease	ice cream	plastic	shoe
polish	bleach	ink	rubber	soap
coffee	linoleum	salad	dye	milk
shampoo				

```
A  C  S  H  A  M  P  O  O  B  L
S  H  O  E  P  O  L  I  S  H  I
A  O  D  F  H  J  K  N  G  E  N
L  R  U  B  B  E  R  K  M  L  O
A  M  I  P  L  A  S  T  I  C  L
D  Y  E  P  E  O  Q  S  L  N  E
T  U  S  O  A  P  U  W  K  V  U
X  A  Z  I  C  E  C  R  E  A  M
C  E  B  D  H  C  O  F  F  E  E
A  X  L  E  G  R  E  A  S  E  Y
```

Look at the word list again.
Put a line under the products you have used.

Name _____

George Washington Carver

Write what you learned about Mr. Carver's life.
Put the information in the order it happened.

_____

_____

_____

_____

_____

_____

_____

_____

How would you describe George Washington Carver? Give reasons for your answer.

_____

_____

_____

Tornado!

Twister, cyclone, and tornado are all names for the same kind of storm. Whatever name you use, it is powerful, frightening, and can cause much damage.

Some of the clouds in the storm grow large and form a funnel shape. The funnel is very thick and usually black. It is formed when cold air rushes up under warm air. The warm air is lighter. It rises quickly and spins around. As the tornado twists, storm winds push it across the land. The small end of the funnel touches down on the earth at times.

The center of the tornado causes a lot of damage. The air pressure in the funnel is much lower than the outside pressure. This makes the tornado act like a giant vacuum cleaner. It can pull trees up by their roots. It can rip the roofs off buildings and toss cars around. Buildings caught by the center of the funnel can explode. There may be lightning, thunder, and heavy rain also.

People who live where tornadoes happen must be prepared. They need a place to go during the storm. Many homes have storm cellars underground where the family stays until the tornado passes.

Almost all tornadoes happen in the United States. They happen most often during spring and early summer. Tornado watchers can give warnings about conditions that might produce a tornado, but the exact location and path cannot be forecast.

Name _____

Questions About *Tornado!*

1. What is a tornado?

   _____

2. Describe a tornado's shape.

   _____

3. What are two other names for a tornado?

   _____

4. How is a tornado like a giant vacuum cleaner?

   _____

5. What kind of damage is caused when a tornado touches the earth?

   _____

6. What must people do after a tornado has done its damage?

   _____

7. Circle the ways to be safe during a tornado.

   run around and scream   go to a storm cellar
   stay away from windows   listen to a battery radio
   stand under a big tree   get in a car and drive away

Think About It

What kind of storms or other natural disasters happen where you live? What kind of damage happens?

_____

_____

_____

_____

Name _____

What Does It Mean?

Match the word with its meaning.

1. pressure	blow up
2. explode	the force of air on a surface
3. lightning	cause harm to something
4. thunder	a place
5. clouds	a collection of water drops suspended in the air
6. damage	electric flashes in the sky
7. cellar	an underground room
8. location	a loud explosion made when lightning flashes

Riddles

Write and draw the answer.

I am a machine used to clean carpets. What am I?	You will see me flashing across the sky in a bad storm. What am I?

_____ | _____

Name _____

Spell *aw*

all • fall   **ough** • bought   **oll** • follow   **aw** • raw

Fill in the missing letters.

1. I have to c_____ my grandfather on his birthday.

2. The wild dogs f_____ over the bones.

3. Squirrels nest in that h_____ tree.

4. Dad used a s_____ to cut the log.

5. Tony bounced his b_____ against the brick w_____.

6. We heard the crows c_____ outside our window.

Base Words

Write the base word on the line.

1. tornadoes   _____

2. lighter   _____

3. touches   _____

4. dried   _____

5. passes   _____

6. scary   _____

7. flies   _____

8. exploding   _____

9. hurried   _____

10. rises   _____

Name _____

Tornado in a Jar

Read the directions.

Materials:

- jar
- water
- liquid detergent (such as Bold)
- small object
  (pebble, Monopoly house, button)

Steps to Follow:

1. Fill the jar almost full of water.
2. Add 1/4 cup of liquid detergent and a small object.
3. Put the lid on securely. Hold the jar with both hands. Shake the jar in a circular motion. Watch the tornado appear.

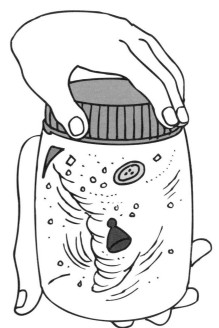

Answer the questions.

1. How many materials do you need? _____

2. What do you do after you put water in the jar?

_____

3. What happens when you shake the jar in a circular motion?

_____

4. Why do you put a small object into the jar?

_____

Now collect your materials and make your own "tornado in a jar."

Answer Key

Page 5
1. squeaky, creaky, shiny
2. leaky, brown
3. The shoes leaked. Or
   They were old and torn.
4. Answers will vary. Might include:
   They were more comfortable.
   I liked the way they looked.
   They were my favorite shoes.
5. squeaky - creaky, leaky
   away - today

Page 6
1. leaky
2. shiny
3. creaky, squeaky
4. they're
5. I've
6. old
7. wear
8. throw away
9. wish
On My Feet - Answers will vary.

Page 7
threw	three	thrush
throat	thread	threat
through	thrill	throb

1. throat
2. threw
3. thread
4. through
5. three
6. thrush

1. peak
2. sneak
3. beak
4. weak
5. squeak
6. leak
7. speak
8. creak

Page 8
1. bear   4. through   7. byte
2. scent   5. bury   8. dough
3. flee   6. rain   9. maize

1. rain   5. dough
2. bear berry   6. board
3. knew   7. heel
4. sow   8. sent

Page 9
Answers will vary.

Page 12
1. She lived at the edge of the woods.
2. She walked on the path across the woods
3. wolf   snake   bear
   They wanted to eat her.
4. She ate and took a nap.
5. She got in the pumpkin to hide from the animals.
6. Answers will vary - should contain...
She tricked the animals into letting her go to her son's house.
She hid in the pumpkin so the animals couldn't see her.
She got them to fight while she got away.

Page 13
old — lived a long time
wise — knows things
giant — very big
path — place to walk
skin and bones — not fat
began — started
broke — fell apart
edge — along the outside
woods — big bunch of trees
hungry — need food

woman   **wolf**
old   bushy-tailed
skin and bones   hungry
wise   gray

snake   **bear**
hungry   big
green   black
long   hungry

Page 14
1. g   5. j
2. j   6. g
3. g   7. j
4. g   8. g

gum   jam jar   giant
jacks   jeep   gorilla

1. son's   3. wolf's   5. tree's
2. woman's   4. pumpkin's   6. bear's

Page 15
The old woman filled a basket with cookies.
She went down the path into the woods.

She met a wolf, a snake, and a bear. "Wait until I come back. I'll be fatter," she said.

The old woman ate and took a nap at her son's house.

The old woman got into the giant pumpkin.
She rolled down the path into the woods.

The pumpkin rolled past the bear, the snake, and the wolf.

The pumpkin rolled into a big tree. It broke open and the old woman fell out.

As the animals began to fight, the old woman ran home.

Page 16
1. She asked the bear to wait.
2. She got into a pumpkin and rolled into the woods.
3. She got them to fight.

Page 19
1. Answers will vary - should include some of these:
   Everything was covered with toys and clothes.
   There was stuff under the bed.
   There was rotten, moldy food.
2. The rotten apple cores, moldy pizza, and dirty clothes.
3. The dust monster wanted to get Herbert to clean his bedroom.
4. It didn't want to smell the rotten food and dirty clothes.
5. Answers will vary.
6. Answers will vary - should include the idea that Herbert threw things around and never put anything away.

Page 20

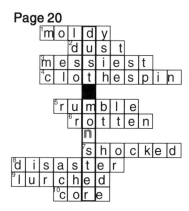

Dust Monster is hiding under the bed.

Page 21

a	e	i	o	u
can	get	ring	dog	hush
that	bed	still	rock	pup
glass	rest	in	bottle	tug
rattle	tell	sing	ball	of

1. smaller   smallest
2. messier   messiest
3. funnier   funniest
4. sillier   silliest
5. faster   fastest
6. tinier   tiniest

Page 22

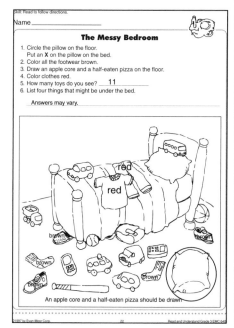

Page 23

Pictures will vary but must include items in the directions.

Page 25

1. They are called nymphs.
2. The eggs are laid in a hole in the ground in the fall.
3. The female grasshopper lays the eggs.
4. A grasshopper molts when it grows too big for its skin
5. nymph   adult   eggs
6. It is a cycle because it happens over and over again. Or
   It is a cycle because the eggs are laid, they grow up, and more eggs are laid.

Page 26

1. Eggs are laid.
2. Nymphs hatch out of the eggs.
3. Nymphs get bigger and grow wings.
4. The grasshopper is grown-up.

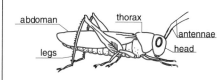

Page 27

adult   the young of some insects
molt   shed skin or feathers
nymph   full-grown
female   to keep on
several   the grasshopper that lays eggs
continue   more than two but not a lot

1. b   2. c   3. a

Page 28

Pictures will vary.
finger   calf   telephone
nymph   coffee   alphabet

laid	came
made	ate
hatched	molted
grew	began
sent	slept

1. sent
2. laid
3. molted   grew
4. ate   came
5. slept   made

Page 29

1. fact
2. opinion
3. fact
4. fact
5. opinion
6. opinion
7. fact

cowgirl	peanut
sunflowers	applesauce
bunkhouse	Grasshopper
breakfast	rainbow
pancakes	sunshine

Page 31

1. Corn, Bean, Squash
2. She is tall, golden, graceful, and strong.
3. She twines around Corn.
4. Squash protects her sisters.
5. The sisters change into girls and dance and sing.
6. Answers will vary - should include some of these:
   Beans, squash, and corn can be planted together.
   The vegetables can grow.
   Bean vines can twine around a corn stalk.
   Corn can be tall and strong.
7. Beans, corn, and squash are not really sisters.
   They can't turn into girls.
   They can't dance in the moonlight.

Page 32
1. Native Americans
2. sisters
3. graceful
4. twine
5. protect
6. praise
7. mound
8. moonlit

corn   bean   squash

Page 33
see   bean   feet
fleas   clean   queen
seed   bean   please

1. see   three
2. clean
3. fleas
4. bean seeds

wanted   planted
loved   stayed
Sentences will vary.

Page 34
stay   youngest
oldest   hate
tall   go
love   short
summer   day
Father   winter
night   Mother

come-go   work-play   small-little
happy-jolly   over-under   dirty-clean
fat-thin   wet-dry   awake-asleep
sad-unhappy   late-early

Page 35
1. Plant them together on one mound.
2. Answers will vary.
3. Answers will vary.

Page 37
1. Kim had not done her homework all week.
2. She could be at the park playing ball and going to Jiffy Burger.
3. Her brother could have ripped it up. She could have been sick.
4. Answers will vary.
5. Answers will vary.

Cause - Kim had not done her homework all week.
Effect - Mother put Kim on restriction.

Page 38
1. drain
2. restriction
3. explain
4. homework
5. trouble
6. groan

1. that's   6. she's
2. doesn't   7. couldn't
3. won't   8. I'll
4. I'm   9. you're
5. They're   10. it's

1. They're   their
2. You're   your
3. it's   its

Page 39
week   noon
sun   thing
some   shine
after   end
over   water
under   sauce
apple   coat
grand   book
skate   parents
note   board

Page 40
1. hope   less
2. slow   ly
3. play   ing
4. explain   s
5. rush   es
6. plan   ing
7. believe   d

1. harmless
2. teacher
3. joyful
4. sadly
5. homeless
6. careful
7. singer
8. quickly

Page 41
Answers will vary - should retell the story in sequence.

Page 44
1. They packed tools, clothes, pots and pans, and mattresses.
2. Pa was going to California to find work.
3. She didn't want to go without her kitten Skeeter.
4. She understood that Laura was unhappy about leaving her home and her pet.
5. Answers will vary - should include some of these:
   Mama explained:
   why they had to go
   they would make a new home in California
   Aunt Lizzie would take good care of the kitten
   they would come back for a visit one day
6. They needed money for the trip.

Page 45
1. mutter
2. huddle
3. cling
4. porch
5. choice
6. determined

1. a   2. b   3. c

Page 46
ways people may speak
explained
cried
muttered
whispered

proper names
Lizzie
Laura
Skeeter

parts of a car
backseat
roof
trunk

members of a family
aunt
brother
parents
sister

©1997 by Evan-Moor Corp.   Read and Understand Grade 3 EMC 640

Page 47

circled words:

open	foam
hello	joke
stone	mower
throat	whole
know	

o-e	open syllable	oa	ow
stone	open		throat know
joke	hello		foam mower
whole			

ed	d	t
headed	begged	washed
wanted	planned	cooked
hunted	traveled	baked
planted	played	picked

Page 48

Problem
They had a flat tire.
Solution
Pa took it to a garage to be fixed.

Problem
They needed gas and food money
Solution
A farmer paid them to pick corn.

Problem
Dog ran away.
Solution
A man found him and brought him back.

Page 50

1. His leg and arm muscles are weak and he is in a wheelchair.
2. Pete went to school for two years.
3. Harry had to learn how to give Pete commands and how to take care of the dog.
4. Answers will vary - could include: pick up things, push wheelchair, open doors, push elevator buttons, turn lights off and on, carry things in a backpack.
5. Pete has to be able to listen to Harry and to do what Harry needs.
6. seeing-eye dog - blind person
   hearing-ear dog - deaf person

Characters - Harry, Pete
Problem - Harry is in a wheelchair and can't do many things for himself.
Solution - Harry gets help from Pete, a service dog.

Page 51

taught
trained
tasks
service-dogs
wheelchair
problems

1. animal	5. drink
2. see	6. small
3. day	7. out
4. swim	8. sleep/lie down

Page 52

stays	knows	drops
pushes	opens	takes
picks	uses	washes

1. stays
2. takes
3. opens
4. knows
5. pushes
6. uses
7. washes
8. picks drops

1. carries	5. worries
2. flies	6. studies
3. hurries	7. tries
4. cries	8. buries

Page 53

book

look	brook
good	hook
cookie	stood

school

smooth	balloon
loose	goose
shampoo	soon

1. closed	opened
2. work	play
3. easy	difficult
4. answer	question
5. pulled	pushed
6. learn	teach
7. under	over
8. laughing	crying

Page 54

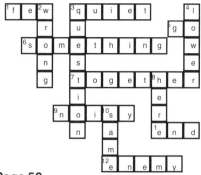

Page 56

1. He is singing to a baby.
2. Answers will vary - could include:
   To help the baby go to sleep.
   To make the baby stop crying.
   To make the baby happy.
3. mockingbird   diamond ring
   looking glass   billy goat
   cart and bull   dog/Rover
   horse and cart
4. a. turn brass
   b. break
   c. turn over
   d. won't bark
5. It is the sweetest baby.

Page 57

(second column answers will vary)
1. bird
2. brass
3. ring
4. town
5. bull

brass-glass   cover-over   broke-goat
fell-bell   bark-cart   buy-fly
you-shoe   come-home   papa-saw

do not
you will
will not
Papa is
cannot
is not
they are
it is
popcorn—The snack is popcorn.

Page 58
kite tie cry
pie dime fry

1. smallest
   smaller
2. faster
   fastest
3. taller
   tallest

Page 59
1. diamond ring
2. mockingbird
3. billy goat
4. buy
5. cart
6. looking glass

mockingbird   cart and horse   baby
diamond ring   looking glass   billy goat

Page 60
Answers will vary.

Page 63
1. He went to the seashore to fish.
2. The fish was magic/enchanted. Or The fish could talk.
3. She kept wanting more things.
4. The fisherman had saved his life. Or The fisherman had put him back in the water.
5. He was angry because she wanted so much/was greedy. He took back everything he had given the fisherman and his wife.
6. She was greedy.
7. Don't be greedy.

Page 64
1. Once upon a time there was a poor fisherman and his wife.
2. The fisherman caught an enchanted fish.
3. His wife sent him to ask for a cottage.
4. His wife sent him to ask for a castle.
5. His wife wanted to rule the world.
6. His wife wanted to rule day and night.
7. The angry fish shouted, "You ask for too much!"
8. The couple were back in their old hut.

Page 65
couple —— a man and a woman who are married
unusual —— satisfied
enchanted —— came in sight
contented —— under a magic spell
greedy —— made the meaning clear
supper —— wanting more than your share
appear —— an evening meal
explain —— strange or rare
rule —— have control over

Pictures will vary.

Page 66
cent-s   candy-k
once-s   magic-k
cereal-s   city-s
canary-k   popcorn-k
fence-s   pancake-k
cut-k   pencil-s

unusual   uncomfortable   unhappy
Sentences will vary.

Page 67
Answers will vary for two-syllable and 3-syllable words.
There are two four-syllable words (vegetables, unusual)

make-believe (any three)
The fish was magic.
The fish could talk.
The fish could grant wishes.
The wife could rule the world.
could really happen (any three)
The man could go fishing.
The woman could work in a garden.
They could live in a hut by the sea.
The wife could be greedy.

Page 69
1. He was complaining that being the middle child wasn't fair. Or
   He was complaining because his big sister and little brother got to do things that he didn't. Or
   He didn't like being the middle child.
2. Answers will vary. (any three from story list)
3. Answers will vary. (any three from story list)

Page 70
1. not fair
2. shop for things, find something to eat.
3. money a parent gives a child
4. say you don't like something
5. old
6. mother, father, grown-ups
Sentences will vary.

Page 71
listen   write   know
talk   climb   sign
1. wrote
2. climbed
3. listened
4. knew

fight   bold
light   cold
night   fold
sight   told
tight   mold

Page 72
Too Young
drive a car
stay out until midnight
work in an office
go to R-rated movies
rent an apartment

I Can Do It
fly a kite
stay overnight with a friend
play soccer
fix my own breakfast
use inline skates

Page 73
Answers will vary.

Page 76
1. Owl started the race.
2. He stopped to take a nap.
3. quick   poky   slow-moving   steady   embarrassed   well-liked   foolish   unkind   show-off
4. Keep trying and you will succeed.

Page 77

1. tortoise
2. congratulated
3. embarrassed
4. crept
5. hare
6. steadily
7. boasted

1. slowly
2. steadily
3. angrily
4. happily

1. steadily   4. slowly
2. messily   5. quickly
3. rapidly   6. angrily

Page 78

bow   goat   bone
sew   hoe   globe
zero   toast   arrow

laugh-f   thought-silent
tough-f   daughter-silent
night-silent   sleigh-silent
cough-f   enough-f
taught-silent   eight-silent

Page 79

Answers will vary - could include:
Hare: "I want to show everyone I am the fastest animal in the world."
Hare: "Tortoise doesn't have a chance. He's the slowest animal there is."

Tortoise: "Hare boasts about how fast he is, but I will outsmart him."
Tortoise: "I plan to move steadily the whole race."

Tortoise: "I knew I had won when I saw Hare taking a nap under a tree."

Page 81

1. Aunt Gertie likes to try new things.
2. You see underwater plants and fish.
3. fins - adds power when you kick your feet
   mask - helps you see underwater
   snorkel - lets you breathe
4. So you will know how to do it safely.

Page 82

places
airport
Hawaiian Islands
hotel
sports center
swimming pool

what you wear
when snorkeling
earplugs
face mask
fins
snorkel
swimsuit

actions
breathe
dive
fly
kick
swim

mask   snorkel   fins

Page 83

I
dive
climbed
dry
buy
fly
Islands

classes   beaches
fins   women
buries   bunnies
men   jets
books   children
dishes   houses
babies   geese
Islands   stories

Page 84

Aunt Gertie said, "Let's have an adventure."
We took classes to learn how to use the equipment.
We bought our own snorkeling equipment.
Aunt Gertie and I flew to the Hawaiian Islands.
We saw fish and plants under the water.
Aunt Gertie is grinning again. What will her next adventure be?

Page 85

1. red circle - 6 lessons $50
2. blue box - Markham Sports Center
3. green line under Saturday
   two green lines under 8:00 -10:00
4. Answers will vary.

Page 88

1. A reptile has dry, scaly skin, lays eggs, and is cold-blooded.
2. Reptiles can't make heat to keep their bodies warm on cold days. They have to live in a place that is warm to stay warm.
3. Any three of these reasons:
   They have eyes and nostrils on top of their head.
   They can close their nostrils to keep out water.
   They have a transparent flap covering their eyes so they can see under water.
   Their color makes it easy for them to hide when they are still.
4. When their teeth fall out they grow new ones right away. Or
   They can grow fifty or more sets of teeth in a lifetime.
5. The mother can hear the babies making noises.
6. crocodile   alligator

Page 89
1. scales
2. animals caught for food
3. a place, an area
4. snake, alligator, turtle
5. hatchling
6. salty water

transparent - clear; can see through it
cold-blooded - can't keep its own body warm

Page 90
word   bird   turn   her   early

My mother is a nurse. Her work is very important. Last Friday afternoon she left work early so we could go to the movies together. But first we ate at the pizza parlor next to the movie theater.

The movie was about a gigantic monster covered in fur. The monster went around the earth frightening everyone.

an alligator	a crocodile	an egg
a nest	a tooth	a pony
an angel	a snout	an orange
a tail	an insect	an octopus

Page 91
1. hard   7. warm
2. happy   8. full
3. small   9. light
4. slow   10. asleep
5. night   11. cooked
6. safe   12. clean

eyes mouth toes nostrils
alligator turtle snake bird
pond river creek stream
capture release trap catch
hat bonnet cap ribbon
chair bench table stool

Page 92

Crocodile and Alligator

Fill in the chart to show the differences between a crocodile and an alligator.

	Crocodile	Alligator
movement on land	move quickly with front and back legs working together	move along on their stomachs with legs spread out at their sides.
snout shape	narrow	round and wide
teeth position	lower tooth shows when mouth is closed	lower tooth doesn't show
nest material and location	digs a nest in the sand	piles up a mound of plant material for a nest

Page 95
1. King Minos controlled the land and the sea.
2. The wings had a wooden frame covered in feathers.
3. He needed to see how they moved their wings and how they hovered on air currents.
4. Icarus flew too near the sun and the heat melted the wax so the feathers fell off his wings.
5. Icarus wouldn't have gotten into trouble if he had followed his father's instruction.
6. Crete and Sicily

Page 96

inventor — creator of new things
soared — rose up in the air
design — make a plan
temptation — something that draws you to it
warning — notice of danger
ignore — to not pay attention
plunge — fall
harm — injure or damage

1. to
2. two
3. too
Sentences will vary.

Page 97
1. oo   9. ow
2. o   10. u
3. ow   11. ow
4. u   12. aw
5. oo   13. oo
6. aw   14. o
7. ow   15. oo
8. o   16. u

design — plan
angry — mad
gather — collect
dangerous — unsafe
middle — center
near — close
harm — injure
joy — happiness
warn — caution
remain — stay
plunge — fall

Page 98
1. moving   hoping   smiling

moves   moved
hopes   hoped
smiles   smiled

2. hopped   hopping
controlled   controlling
planned   planning

hops
controls
plans

3. hurries   hurried
studies   studied
buries   buried

hurrying
studying
burying

Page 99
Effect - Daedalus decided to find a way to leave by air.

Effect - He designed wings to fly off the island.

Effect - The wax melted and he fell into the sea and drowned.

©1997 by Evan-Moor Corp.
Read and Understand Grade 3 EMC 640

Page 102

1. The children had been good all day.
2. They were headed west.
3. She followed a rabbit into the woods.
4. He was funny-looking/strange looking. Or
   He was dressed in old clothes, his feet were bare, and he had on a funny hat.
5. She wasn't afraid because he had a kind smile and a twinkle in his eyes.
6. People started calling him Johnny Appleseed because he gave people apple seeds and little apple trees.
7. Granny planted them with the seeds Johnny Appleseed gave her.
8. Answers will vary.

Page 103

1. traveling
2. staying
3. following
4. raising
5. wishing
6. going

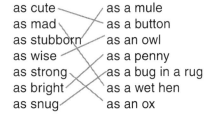

as cute — as a button
as mad — as a wet hen
as stubborn — as a mule
as wise — as an owl
as strong — as a bug in a rug
as bright — as a penny
as snug — as an ox

Page 104

1. a child
2. crying
3. yes
4. noisy commotion
5. want to do or have something
6. people Johnny met
7. very
8. Answers will vary.

Page 105

1. raise   5. afraid
2. table   6. space
3. player   7. crayon
4. plane   8. mayor

1. She   5. them
2. him   6. He
3. it   7. We
4. They   8. them

Page 106

Answers will vary.

Page 108

1. It has fur. Babies are born alive and fed milk from the mother.
2. A koala mother has a pouch where she raises her baby.
3. A koala uses its sharp front teeth to tear off leaves or strip bark. It uses its flat back teeth to chew its food.
4. The koala wedges itself into the fork of a tree and wraps its arms or legs around a branch.
5. Male koalas don't need pouches because they don't have babies.

General statements - Several kinds of marsupials live in Australia. Or Marsupials eat plants.

Page 109

1. mammal
2. female
3. nocturnal
4. pouch
5. wedge
6. marsupials
7. eucalyptus
8. Australia

1. an eucalyptus tree
2. where two branches come together
3. the outside layer of a tree
4. tender new growth on a tree

Page 110

1. fun-ny   5. on-ly
2. ten-der   6. in-to
3. pen-cil   7. mon-ster
4. bas-ket   8. can-dle

1. mother's
2. its
3. boys'
4. men's
5. its
6. children's

1. koala baby's pouch
2. Mario's letter
3. children's cookies
4. its leash
5. captain's ship
6. kittens' toys

Page 111

1. both
2. both
3. both
4. both
5. koala
6. dog
7. koala
8. dog

The only words not circled in the list are: born, koala, slow, pouch, tree

Page 112

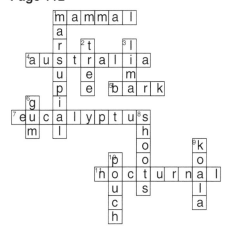

Page 114

1. Mir is the Russian space station.
2. Two Russian cosmonauts were on board.
3. Answers will vary - could contain:
   She was born in Shanghai, China. Her parents were missionaries. She grew up in Oklahoma. She wanted to be a space explorer.
4. She learned to fly an airplane and she studied science in college.
5. She sent them e-mail messages every day.
6. She exercised every day to see if this would keep her bones and muscles strong.
7. Yes. She wants to go to Mars next.

©1997 by Evan-Moor Corp.

Read and Understand Grade 3 EMC 640

Page 115
1. Mir
2. astronaut
3. Shanghai
4. weightless
5. cosmonaut
6. exercise
7. wobbly
8. space station
9. missionary

1. in Shanghai, China.
2. Oklahoma.
3. fly a plane.
4. science in college.
5. female astronauts in America.
6. in space on the Mir space station.
7. go to Mars.

Page 116

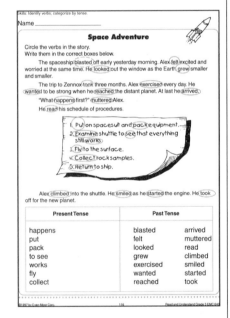

Page 117
Answers will vary.

Page 118
1. unable
2. joyful
3. weightless
4. pregame
5. unhappy
6. preview
7. beautiful
8 penniless
Sentences will vary.

Page 120
1. Eli watched a scary movie about vampires.
2. Answers will vary - should include some of these:
Bats can fly.
Vampire bats are small.
Vampire bats eat blood.
They have razor sharp teeth.
They can carry rabies.
They live in warm tropical places.
They sleep during the day and eat at night.
They usually don't bite humans.
They don't suck up blood; they lap it up.
3. They can carry diseases.
4. Answers will vary - could include:
Call 911.
Tell your parents.
Go to the doctor.

Page 121
1. they-a
2. time-i
3. scream-e
4. night-i
5. go-o
6. sleep-e
7. day-a
8. though-o
9. movie-e
10. cute-u
11. cloak-o
12. fly-i
13. human-u
14. strain-a

long a	long e	long o
ey	ea	ough
ay	ee	oa
ai	ie	o

long i	long u
i-e	u-e
igh	u
y	

1. e   4. e
2. i   5. i
3. e   6. i

one-syllable words - i
two-syllable words - e

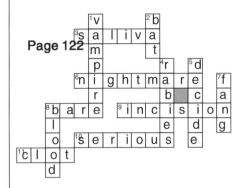

Page 122

Page 123
1. true
2. false
3. true
4. false
5. true
6. true
7. false
8. true
9. false

Page 124
Answers will vary - could include:
birds only
lay eggs
eat seeds and insects
are covered in feathers
both birds and vampire bats
fly
take care of their babies
vampire bats only
are covered in fur
have live babies
feed their babies milk

Page 126
1. His real mother was stolen. He and his brother were left behind.
2. seven - knew about plants; was called "plant doctor"
ten - ran away to find a school he could go to
1890 - began college
3. Thomas Edison wanted Mr. Carver to work in his laboratory. He had other plans.
4. He developed ways to use peanuts and sweet potatoes so they could grow something besides cotton.
5. He started an agricultural department.
6. He got his nickname because of all his inventions with peanuts and sweet potatoes.
7. Missouri, Kansas, Alabama

©1997 by Evan-Moor Corp.
Read and Understand Grade 3 EMC 640